AS TIME GOES BY

1900s

David Noble

The High Street, Oldland Common from a drawing
by Samuel Loxton © 1912.

A PICTORIAL AND TEXT PRESENTATION
OF COMMUNITY LIFE
FROM THE 1900's TO 1990's
IN OLDLAND COMMON, NORTH COMMON,
BRIDGEYATE AND BITTON
IN
BRISTOL AVON

ABOUT THE PHOTOGRAPHER

Robert Lewis

Robert, born in 1960, was educated at the local Oldland Schools of St Anne's Primary and Sir Bernard Lovell. He spent two years at Soundwell Technical College followed by three years studying for a degree in Accountancy and Law at University in Cardiff.

Robert's interest in photography began at an early age, following on from his grandfather's enthusiasm for the subject in earlier years. Robert is a member of Kingswood Photographic Society, of which his grandfather, Malcolm Meredith, was a founder member.

Robert has recently started a series of local postcards depicting village scenes. He is also an enthusiastic entrant in the Oldland Horticultural Society village show and won first prize in each of the photographic competition categories at this year's show.

Robert is able to develop his interest in photography in his work as a Chartered Accountant for, Robson Taylor, a firm located in Bath. He has undertaken several photographic assignments for the firm in producing marketing and other literature.

First published in 1993 by
David and Marguerite Noble
Damar House
27 Longmoor Road
Ashton Gate
Bristol
BS3 2NZ
Tel. 0272–669556

ISBN 0 9517648 1 0

Cover design by Andrew Wilkey, Graphic Design of Keynsham, Bristol.

Cover Photographs by Robert Lewis – 1993 and centre drawing by S Loxton – 1912 of Jefferies Court, Castle Road, Oldland Common.

Typeset by "Anneset", Weston-super-Mare, Avon.

Printed in Great Britain.

DEDICATION

FOREWORD

David has put together an enjoyable 'read' of true local history. Seeing some of the photographs of yester-year gave me a great feeling of nostalgia. My mind drifted back to the days of long, warm summers, when the special day of the year came round – the Sunday School outing to Weston Super Mare! Everyone gathered outside the Methodist Chapel in West Street, Oldland Common and eagerly awaited the arrival of the Princess Mary Touring Coaches and a shout of glee was heard as the coach was spotted coming from Cowhorn Hill. What excitement!

I remembered too the bonfires and fireworks on VE and VJ days, the skies red with celebrations and the piano playing merrily on the Union Inn (now the Cherry Tree) car park – the war was over! Memories of picnics in the Glen, delightful walks from Oldland to Keynsham tea gardens where we would hire a boat and row up the Avon to Saltford. Adventure was the name of the game in the summer holidays and this meant visits to Grannie's Rocks, Pipley Bottom or Catscliffe.

Thankyou for reviving many happy memories David in your first book 'An Oldland Boy Looks Back' and may I wish you every success with this new publication and any future books in the series. I am sure that this book will not only revive many memories for older residents, but will also give an insight to young people and 'newcomers' into life, as it was, in their particular village.

Malcolm Bridge

Malcolm Bridge, Former Chairman of Bitton Parish and member of Kingswood Borough Councils.

ACKNOWLEDGEMENTS

The production of this book would not have been possible without the valued help of many people and organisations.

I would like to express my sincere thanks particularly to my wife, Marguerite for patiently typing and editing the manuscript and for her continuous support throughout; to Robert Lewis of High Street, Oldland Common for all his photographic skill, advice and availability and to all those who so willingly made a personal contribution to this publication.

Ian Allan Ltd – Shepperton. (Railway photograph).

Automobile Association.

Avon Valley Railway, Bitton.

Bristol Central Reference Library.

Bristol Evening Post (Bristol United Press Ltd).

Bristol Observer (Bristol United Press Ltd).

Mrs Doreen Buckee of Hanham.

By Gone Bristol – Derek and Janet Fisher.

John Channing – Pickwick Portraits of Keynsham.

Chronicle Communication Ltd.

Roger Clarke of Keynsham for photographs.

Mr Patrick Conroy – Planning Officer, Kingswood Borough Council.

Brian Davies – Secretary of Fry's Sports and Social Club.

George Gregory – of St. Anne's for photograph.

Home Publishing Company Ltd. (A Member of McMillan Group PLC).

Mrs Eileen Noble. of Cadbury Heath

Ordnance Survey.

Readers Digest.

Redcliffe Press Ltd (Bristol).

Gloucestershire County Council.

Councillor Roy Stone – (Former Mayor of Kingswood Borough Council).

Ken Thomas – Archivist of Courage Ltd – Information on the public houses.

Rev Kenneth Thomas – former Vicar of Oldland 1953/71.

Mike Tozer of Pill, Bristol – Photographs from the 'M J Tozer Collection'.

Paul and Jill Willmott – Authors of 'Through The Years' local publication.

Representatives and members of all the Churches.

Heads and members of staff of all the schools.

Landlords and Landladies of all the public houses.

Representatives of all the Community Organisations.

Residents of the various villages for their invaluable help.

Oldland Common – Betty Clarke (Oldland W.I.), Jean Hireson (Photographs and information), Christine Deacon, Mr Phillips and Mr Stanley (Sir Bernard Lovell School), Brenda Andrews (Oldland United Choir), Audrey Mitchell (Oldland Players).

North Common – Molly Hathway, Roger and Carol Fowler, Albert Lansdale.

Bridgeyate – Pete and Maureen Wiltshire, Rex Whittock.

Bitton – Gordon and Joan Neal (now of Oldland Common), Joyce Gerrish, Jenny Powell, Charlie Hurst, Sandra Veasey and Edna Nelmes.

CONTENTS

Chapter	Title	Page
	Introduction	vi
1	Oldland Common, Past and Present	1
2	The Changing Scene of North Common	35
3	'Through The Decades'	61
4	Around and About Bridgeyate	81
5	Bitton, Yesterday and Today	95
	Listed Buildings in the Locality	121
	Postscript	122
	Bibliography	122

INTRODUCTION

Following the encouraging reception and interest shown in my first publication, 'An Oldland Boy Looks Back', a number of people have commented on how much they enjoyed reading about the earlier days in Oldland Common and that looking back had revived many happy memories for them.

In response to this interest I have produced 'As Time Goes By' which I hope will be the first in a series of pictorial and text presentations of Oldland Common and its neighbouring villages. It features scenes which reflect life as it was within the community from the beginning of the century with comparable views as they are today.

The villages of Oldland Common, North Common, Bridgeyate and Bitton, like many rural areas in Avon and indeed throughout the Country have changed in many respects over the years. Old buildings have been pulled down for modernisation, open farmland has been replaced to make way for housing estates and the many old roads have been widened to cope with the increased volume of traffic. It could be so rightly said that many aspects of village life have taken on a 'new look'. There are some village folk who may comment that village life "Aint what it used to be" and would much prefer to return to those 'good old days' when life was lived at a much slower pace. Many villagers however, have accepted the changes which had to be made in order to facilitate progress. Whatever the 'achievements' of today, these can be looked upon, especially by the younger element within the community, as the 'memories of tomorrow'.

A popular feature with many readers in 'An Oldland Boy Looks Back' was the chapter entitled, 'O Yes we remember it well'. It highlighted the many activities and events which transpired during the 1940's to 1960's and also gave the opportunity for four local residents of the day to recall some of their memories of 'life in Oldland Common'. In this publication I have aimed to include more resident participation, for I believe that the people themselves are the main contributors to the memories of village life. Whilst interviewing and talking to many people over the past five years or so, I have enjoyed listening to the varied and descriptive accounts of their own personal experiences of village life within the community. I am therefore very grateful to all those who have so willingly contributed toward these sections which are located at the end of each appropriate chapter.

In between the chapters on North Common and Bridgeyate I have included a section called 'Through the Decades' which gives some dates of interest both locally, nationally and internationally from the 1900's to 1990's.

It has been the intention in this book to specifically illustrate the transition through which village life has passed over the years. It is therefore hoped that the contents have given an equal balance of information which I trust will capture the imagination of the reader in 'AS TIME GOES BY'.

OLDLAND COMMON
PAST AND PRESENT

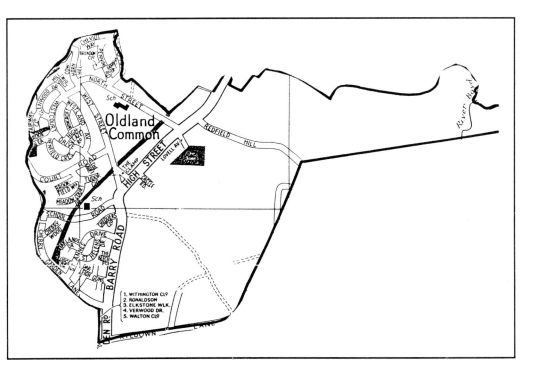

Map of Oldland Common in the Borough of Kingswood – 1993

1

OLDLAND COMMON, as it's name suggests, has been cultivated for a long time. It was part of the Kingswood Forest and was first mentioned in the Domesday Book of 1086 as 'Aldelande'. The name derives from the Old English *Ald* and *land* meaning an 'old tract of land' or in other words, an old piece of land which has been long in use. Samuel Rudder in his County History 1779 says about the Oldland district, '*it is beautifully varied with easy elevations and some bolder rising ground. . . The greater part is meadow and pasture both in common fields and enclosures'*. During the Roman period it is recorded that the Romans passed through Oldland on their way to Bath.

The village of Oldland, incorporating Oldland Common, was set out as a triangle of streets, High Street, West Street and North Street surrounding the common fields or old tract of land. Several smaller roads led from the main streets and since the 1950's these have increased in number and importance due to the various housing developments replacing the open farm land and demolishing many of the old cottages.

In the 18th century the population of the area started to increase and that is when Oldland began to take shape around 'the Common'. The population of the village in 1901 was 1,956 and in the early 1930's it was 2,125. By the mid to late 1950's it was 2,750 and in the 1980's and early 1990's it peaked at around 3,200.

Ever since the middle of the last century the village has had two primary schools, St Anne's, formerly the Church of England School and Oldland Council School, now Redfield Edge. In 1951 Oldland Common Secondary Modern School was opened in the High Street. The girls of this school moved, in 1956, to new premises in North Street. In 1968 both schools were renamed and became known as Sir Bernard Lovell School for boys and girls. So named after the well known astronomer and Director of Jodrell Bank Experimental Station in Cheshire, who was born in Oldland. The two schools amalgamated in September 1971 to become a mixed comprehensive school located in the former girls school in North Street. In September 1980 a completely new school, Cherry Garden Primary, was opened in Cherry Garden Lane.

During this century the community has been fortunate to be served by five churches, four public houses and two public halls. The Parish Church of St Anne's on the hill overlooking Oldland Vale; The Congregational Church (now the United Reformed Church) and The Brethren Gospel Hall both in the High Street; The Methodist Church in West Street and the Brethren Meeting Room in Cloverlea Road which closed it's doors as a place of worship in July 1973.

The local pubs were The Dolphin Inn, in the High Street; The Union Inn (now the Cherry Tree) on the junction of High Street and West Street; The Crown and Horseshoe at the top of North Street and The Greyhound situated in West Street which closed as a licensed premises in July 1958.

The Church and Village Halls both built in 1913 have been greatly used for local events in the community over the years.

In a traditional rural village such as Oldland, farming was one of the main industries. For most of this century, particularly up to the 1960's open farmland was occupied by numerous farms. There were as many as nine general farms, two poultry farms, three small holdings and three market gardens. Only some of these farms remain today. Some have been converted to other uses and some have completely disappeared in the extensive housing developments which have taken place.

In addition to the farms and all the various shops scattered around the village other industries have also had a large part to play. Probably the best known village industry around the turn of this century was boot and shoe making. Two factories, one in High Street and the other in North Street, were in operation 'on the Common' as well as the numerous 'home workers' involved in the industry working away in small workshops in their back gardens. Both factories ceased production prior to the Second World War with the general decline in the boot and shoe trade in the district. They subsequently became the Candle Factory/Pybus' Washing Powder and *Stanfords Furnishers respectively.

In the late 18th and early 19th century when the population of Oldland was beginning to grow an influx of Flemish refugees to the Cowhorn Hill area, brought with them the industry of felt and beaver hat making. These workers were known as the 'Hatters' and gave local families the opportunity for a profitable living.

Another industry situated in the High Street at the turn of the century was corset making and the factory was owned by Messrs. Chas Bayer & Company and employed 200 people. During the Second World War it became a tank factory and then later Cox's Engineering. In the 1950's it was owned by Oldland Motorbody Builders which closed in the mid 1970's. It has subsequently been owned by Simplex Sectional Bookcases. Most of the industry of the village today is centred around this area with the emphasis on light engineering and a small industrial estate.

Mining was an industry much in evidence in the area since the 13th Century and relics of it can be seen to this day. California Colliery in California Road was the last colliery to close in 1904 due to flooding.

Although some of Oldland's landmarks remain many of the old cottages have been demolished or modernised. The streets have taken on a new look and former residents returning to Oldland have difficulty in recognising the old familiar places. However, it has still retained some of it's characteristics and these can be seen in the following 'old' and 'new' photographs together with a number of past and present community activities.

More detailed information about Oldland can be found in 'An Oldland Boy Looks Back' published by the author in 1991.

*Footnote: The Stanford's building in North Street was demolished this year, on 21st July 1993.

All adverts in this publication relate to occupants/owners during 1950's/60's.

A tranquil village scene. High Street in the 1920's with a delivery cart parked near the old Post Office. The population of Oldland Common at this time was about 2,000.
Photograph supplied by 'Bygone Bristol'.

The same scene in 1993. The village Post Office is now located on the corner of Castle Road and High Street and is owned by Barry and Janet Thearle. Bristol Drapers owned by Ron and Greta Pearce occupies the old Post Office premises. Heavy traffic uses the busy High Street. The population today is about 3,200.
Photograph by Robert Lewis of High Street, Oldland Common. All photographs in this publication were taken by Robert Lewis unless otherwise indicated.

West Street from the railway bridge during the turn of the century. The open land of the Common before the Village Hall of today was built and on the left hand side can be seen the sign for the Greyhound Inn, Rose Cottage, Adam's shop and Oldland Methodist Church.
Photograph supplied by Roy Stone of Cadbury Heath.

The Village Hall just visible through the trees on the right. Private houses on the left replace the Greyhound Inn.

Photograph taken in 1922. Two cottages built in 1825 on the corner of North Street and West Street. The Crown and Horseshoe Public House is in the background.
Photograph from the M J Tozer Collection.

Pictured outside the enchanting Crown Cottage, the above two cottages made into one, is Pauline Scrase who together with her husband now own these premises. David and Pauline were formerly the Landlord and Landlady of the Crown and Horseshoe which has been re-modernised over recent years.

The Greyhound Inn which was situated in West Steet but closed in 1958
Photograph courtesy of Courage Ltd.

Privately owned homes are now built on the land where the Greyhound Inn once stood.

This Samuel Loxton Drawing (1912) is of Jefferies Court in Castle Road also known to many locals as Moses Lane. Some well known Oldland names of families who lived in this area during the 40's and 50's were, Linton, Beavis, Hamblin, Brain, Fuller, Teal, Brewer, Saunders and Luffman. The cottages were built before the turn of the century by a Mr Jefferies after whom the Court was named. He actually lived in one of the cottages in the Court during the same period.

Not a trace of the old buildings today. This modern bungalow, the home of Connie and Ray Isaacs, is set in beautiful surroundings where Jefferies Court used to be in 1955.

The building of the Village Hall in 1913. The Hall was officially opened the following year in 1914.

Photograph supplied by Roy Stone of Cadbury Heath.

The Village Hall today remains a focal point and a hive of activity with a variety of events held there.

A quiet fold in the green hills relieved by the mellow stonework of rural cottages and an old bridge. Taken from the foot of the drive leading to St Anne's Parish Church in February 1962.
Photograph by Courtesy of The Bristol Observer.

The same view from the same spot in 1993. Now surrounded by trees and shrubs, the old road bridge, which was partially demolished by the floods of 1968 has been replaced by a wooden footbridge.

Oldland Common Station photographed in 1948. The Station was opened on the 2nd December 1935 and closed on 6th March 1966. The Railway had a frequent passenger service between Bristol and Bath from before the start of the Century until 1966. The first person to buy a ticket from the station in 1935 was Mr Tom Woodman.
Photograph courtesy of Ian Allan Ltd.

The Railway track as it is today. The area alongside the old track is now the Cycle-path and walkway. On the 6th March 1991, exactly 25 years to the day that the last passenger trains ran between Bristol and Bath, an extension of the Bitton to Oldand Common Railway was re-opened by the Mayor of Kingswood Borough Council, Councillor George Rogers on behalf of Avon Valley Railway.

A A Adams shop in the High Street was owned by Eric and Barbara Adams and closed for business in the early 1970's.

The same location in 1993 but now 'Redland House' – flats which are occupied by many well known Oldland families.

Oldland Council School – Juniors 1948/49.
Back row; David Kendall, Gloria Woodman, Christine Saunders, Molly Hathway, Eunice Morgan, Doris Gay, Kathleen Smart, Clive Britton, Robert Willmott, Timothy Robottom, Stephen Luddington and Keith Milward.
Middle row; Kathleen Gay, Betty Field, Gillian Luddington, Tony Beavis, Miss Hill (class teacher), Barry Butt, Freddie Lewis, Myrtle Slade, and Iris Stride.
Front row; Alan King, Peter Linton, Tony Martin, Ann Fowler, Marguerite Upward, Vivienne Gurney and Robin Phelps.
Photograph supplied by Molly Hathway, Bath Road, North Common

Class 7 of Redfield Edge Primary School 1993 (formerly Oldland Council School) photographed with their teacher Miss Louise Hillier
Photograph courtesy of John Channing, Pickwick portraits of Keynsham

13

The Senior Class of Oldland Secondary Modern School for Girls located in North Street – 1958.
Photograph supplied by Joy Matthews (Nee Gilman) of Keynsham pictured third from left on the front row.

Year 11 (5th Year) Pupils of the same school photographed in 1993. The school was renamed Sir Bernard Lovell School in 1968. The Boys and Girls Schools amalgamated in September 1971. The School currently has some 900 pupils on the roll.
Photograph supplied by Christine Deacon of Meadow Court Drive.

Oldland Secondary Modern School Football XI, season 1955/56 pictured with Sportsmaster Mr W Brown. Back row: D England, R Morgan, M Smith, C Willmott, C Stone, R Willmott. Front row: T Davies, D Jerwood, B Johnson(Capt), C Turner, R Turner.
Photograph supplied by Mr W Brown of Hanham.

Oldland Church of England School Football X1 Season 1964/65. Pictured with Mr J Angell (Headmaster), Mr Don Jay and Mr Taylor.
Photograph supplied by Rev Kenneth Thomas, former vicar of Oldland 1953/71.

15

Pupils of Oldland Church of England School (St Annes'), Junior class photographed, with their teacher Miss Taylor, in 1960 on 'the bank' of the school playing field.
Photograph supplied by Steve Phelps, formerly of West Street now of St George, pictured extreme left on back row.

Pupils of Class V 3/4, Miss Veal's Class of the same school in 1993, photographed outside the school swimming pool.

Staff of Mr A Lockwood's Nursery – Highfields, Cherry Garden Lane, taken during the blitz in 1940. Included in the photograph are some well known Oldland family names:- Frank Morgan,- Henry Weeks, Fred Coles, Cressy and Ernest Hicks.
Photograph supplied by Ken Hicks of Cherry Garden Lane.

Staff of 'The Corset Factory' pictured in the 1920's outside the factory situated in the High Street, where Simplex Sectional Bookcases is today.
Photograph supplied by Jean Hireson of West Street.

OLDLAND COMMON AND IT'S COMMUNITY

Oldland Drama Group presented 'Beside the Seaside' in October 1958 and the cast are pictured during rehearsals in the Church Hall.
Photograph supplied by Rev Kenneth Thomas.

Members of Oldland Methodist Players presenting an Operetta entitled 'The Magic Key' held in the Village Hall in 1938. Cast pictured left to right: Flo Davis, Desmond Fudge, Majorie Hall, Edna Brain, Ivy Wake, Ron Fudge, Norah Phelps, Ernest Phelps, Ivy Saunders, Ellen Butler, Ivy Davies and Elsie Holder.
Photograph supplied by Ernest and Norah Phelps of West Street.

The Oldland Players take a break during the dress rehearsal of their 3rd production, 'And So To Bed', held in the Church Hall in 1968

Photographed on stage in 1991 for the Players 48th production, 'Look Who's Talking' are; Left to right – Jill Gregory, Jim McLaughlin, Janice Howes, David Walford and Mary Mason.

Photographs supplied by Audrey Mitchell of Court Road a founder member of the group who has been involved in every production since it's commencement in 1967. She writes the following on the occasion of their 50th production, 'Old Time Music Hall', held in 1992.

"Imagine the scene – the year is 1967 and the first committee of the newly formed Oldland Players choose the first play, 'Watch it Sailor'. Auditions are duly held – a few weeks into rehearsal and the actress playing the role of the spinster Auntie tells the producer she is going to be a mother (nicely put). Well the group overcome the problem – the play was greeted with delight by the village and the Players were here to stay.

The membership like that of any group, fluctuates and some years the numbers of members can be quite low, which does restrict the type of play which can be given. Over the years the group have had approximately 135 members who have joined them. It is the past members as well as the present that have made the group what it is today – well known in Amateur Drama. We are grateful for all they gave to the group and remember them as we celebrate what we started 25 years ago."

Oldland Flower Show Committee Members 1921.
Photograph supplied by Jean Hireson of West Street.

Committee Members of Oldland Horticultural Society pictured on the day of the 20th Annual Show held at St Anne's School Field on August 28th 1993.

Oldland United Churches Whit Monday Procession around the Village in 1961. The Photograph shows the Fishponds British Legion Band heading the procession along West Street.
Photograph supplied by the Rev Kenneth Thomas.

Members and friends of Oldland Brethren Gospel Hall pictured at the 'Tent' meeting held in Mr Jarrett's field at the top of the High Street in the 1930's. This was situated near to where the Gospel Hall is today.
Photograph supplied by Albert Lansdale of North Common.

Villagers and Friends of Oldland St Anne's Church gathered at the Christmas Fair held in the Church Hall in 1958.
Photograph supplied by the Rev Kenneth Thomas.

Members of the Oldland Women's Institute gathered with local councillors on the corner of School Road during the presentation of a seat to the village in June 1966.
Photograph supplied by the Secretary of the WI Betty Clark of North Street.

The Oldland Churches United Choir performing during their musical production of 'Pharoah to Freedom' held at the Methodist Church in the late 1980's
Photograph supplied by Brenda Andrews of North Common.

The Conductor of the Oldland United Choir Brenda Andrews and her daughter, pianist Sharon Gilborson.
Photograph supplied by Brenda Andrews.

The Oldland United Choir was formed in 1982 and consists of members from each of the Oldland Churches. Over the past 11 years the membership of the choir has gradually increased from about 30 to it's present 50. During this time the Choir has performed nine different musicals with 'Pharoah to Freedom' being the most popular having been performed in many churches throughout the area over a period of two years.

As well as giving much joy to both singer and listener alike the home performances have raised £1,995 for charity. All the members of the group enjoy the Christian fellowship thus making it a truly 'United Choir'.

Oldland Cricket 1st X1 pictured in 1921. In those earlier years of the century Oldland Cricket Club played their matches on one of Mr Upwards' fields on Cowhorn Hill before transferring to the 'Rec' in Castle Road in the 40's.
Photograph supplied by Jean Hireson of West Street, daughter-in-law of the Team Captain Percy Hireson seated centre of the middle row.

Oldland St Anne's AFC 1921/22 season. Team Members during this season in position order were:- C Mortimor, J Anstey, C Harding, F Saunders, L Jay, S Lear, C Mortimor, J Pride, W Hunt, R Mortimor, E Dobson and C Saunders.
M J Tozer collection.

Oldland Football Club. Amongst one of the most memorable achievements of the Football Club was the winning of the Gloucestershire FA Senior Cup in the 1976/77 season. Pictured on this occasion are the successful team and Club officials.
Photograph supplied by Gordon Harvey of North Common, former Chairman of Oldland FC.

Oldland Football Club 1992/93 Season. Back row: R Sealey (Manager), J Haberfield, K Gleeson, D Winstone, A Boulton, S Cains, I Davidson, J Morgan, M Hawkins, S Painter, H Johnson (Chairman)
Front Row: I Hyett, M Willmott, M Rennie, M Burt, S Pruett, A Williams, M Wheeler
Photograph supplied by Reg Hamblin who has served the club loyally for over 40 years

REFLECTIONS ON LIFE AS IT WAS IN OLDLAND COMMON IN THE 1930's

by
Allan Taylor
formerly of North Street,
Oldland Common, now of Winterton,
Scunthorpe, Humberside

The Taylor Family in 1942, left to right Eileen, Ivan, Mrs Lilian Taylor, Allan, Margaret, Frank, Patricia and Pamela.

My Father had a bungalow built, near the station known as 'The Halt', in 1933/34 on a three acre field, one acre of which we cultivated by hand. At that time I was 10 years old and had two brothers and four sisters. We soon made friends with the local lads, namely, Dick and Jim Gerrish, Claude Hireson, Gilbert Lucas and Harold Summerill to name but a few.

Oldland Station was built in 1935 and I remember some of the locals walking to Bitton Station just to catch the first train to stop at Oldland. The station was run by one man, Mr Arthur Packer from his little wooden ticket office and his stove was heated with coal supplied by the various engines stopping at the station. The railway was then the London, Midland and Scottish Railway (L.M.S). After the railway station opened, it became quite a family concern. We became friendly with the drivers, firemen and guards as members of our family used the trains every day to travel to St Phillips Station in Bristol, and invariably one or other of us was late and chased down the embankment to catch the train as it was moving out, accompanied with whistles from the engine and whoops from the driver.

One winter we had a bad storm with very high winds and at about 3.00am in the morning there was a banging on the door and a voice shouting to my father, "wake up Fred one of your sheds has blown down on the line." We all got up and with the help of the driver and fireman carried the remains back up to the top of the embankment. Happy days!

The school in the village when we arrived in 1934/35 was the 'Elementary' or Council School run by the Headmaster, Mr 'Sammy' Uglow and two of the teachers, Mr 'Mickey' Smith and Miss Jones. I believe that Mr Smith and Miss Jones eventually married.

I vividly remember the 'Rec' (recreation field) in Castle Road being opened in 1937 by Mr and Mrs Atchison. All we children had our photograph taken at the time sitting on a rocking horse and I was asked to hold someone's baby for the picture.

The village hall is a building which holds a lot of memories for me. Our Scout Headquarters was situated behind the hall in a wooden shed. The Scoutmaster then was Mr Day, a Canadian, who was, as I remember, a first class teacher and certainly held our attention especially in Woodcraft and Forestry. Our uniforms were green shirts and black and yellow neckerchiefs and we were quite proud of them.

Another delight held in the hall was the occasional 'magic lantern show'. These were quite a novelty then.

The village hall was also used as the headquarters, for our 'Homeguard', namely the 6th Glosters and after training we usually made our way to 'The Greyhound' Pub for some scrumpy. I think one of the funniest things I can remember, in the initial stages of the 'Homeguard', was the line of men when we were on 'parade' at the back of the village hall. It was 'Dad's Army' in the making! The ages varied between 16 and 70 years. Some in part uniform and some in civvies. Weights varying from 8 stone to 17 stone and heights between 5ft and 6'6". Armed to the teeth, carrying a sweeping brush handle with a kitchen knife tied to the end and all under the orders of the local Undertaker, Mr Merrett as Captain! I remember one Saturday night, when we were using the skittle alley as our headquarters, a dance was in progress upstairs and one of the 'Homeguardsmen' accidentally fired his rifle straight through the ceiling of the skittle alley! Luckily it missed everyone at the dance. One Sunday, in training, we were scheduled to attack Colerne Aerodrome in conjunction with several Platoons from around the district. It was planned down to the last detail. Transport to Wick, then advance towards Colerne finally going through some woods until the outer perimeter of the 'Drome was reached. We were led by Sgt. Hamblin (of Redfield Hill). He told us to wait while he went to investigate but we never saw him again until after the operation because he was captured. However, we carried on regardless ably assisted by two Hawker Hurricanes dropping sand bags on the barbed wire entanglements. We eventually finished with a 'set to' with the groundstaff who were thoroughly disgruntled at being turned out of bed on a Sunday morning!

Before the war broke out, my father with our help, built our own air raid shelter, quite sizeable to take the whole family. I remember during the twelve hour blitz on Bristol one Sunday night, whilst in the shelter we heard a whole series of 'plops'. Looking out we were astonished to see incendary bombs burning all around us, we ran around trying to cover them up with earth in case they attracted H.E.bombs. The next day we found a large hole in the field. On another occasion during the night three bombs were jettisoned by a German bomber and one exploded at the back of the Dolphin Pub in the High Street, in the soft ground alongside a cottage, blowing it's roof off. The old man living in the cottage had been in a heavy sleep after spending the previous evening in the Pub and was still asleep when the neighbours turned up! My memory takes me back to the factory opposite the Dolphin Pub. At the beginning of the war they used to make bullet proof petrol tanks for aircraft. These were made of various types of rubber, laminated to self seal if a bullet went through.

A person I would like to mention is Ron Painter who was the local butcher's boy before Ford and Darby took over the business. He used to deliver meat around the village on a bicycle with a large basket on the front. He was full of 'devilment' and many a time he used to lift the front wheel of his bike in the air and do a 'wheelie' and of course occasionally the meat fell out onto the road. He became a Squadron Leader Bomber Pilot in the RAF and after a complete tour of Operations was detailed to fly the comedian 'Wee Georgie Wood' to various parts of the world for troop concerts.

Whilst still at school, I found myself a part time job delivering milk in 1 pint cans for Morgan's farm – the farm house is still in North Street. I remember that their cattle used to graze in the field where Sir Bernard Lovell School is now situated. My wage was 2/6d (12½p) plus ½ pint of clotted cream from the one Jersey cow on the farm. Needless to say I was nearly always late for school!

About 5 years ago having visited Bristol on business, I spent an afternoon in Oldland having a look around. My word what a change! I finally went up Redfield Hill and down into Beach where as children we spent many happy hours. I stopped on the bridge and savoured the peace and tranquility, listening to the birds and the ripple of the stream, (River Boyd) my memory taking me back to those early days. I must admit it brought a tear to my eyes. What a lovely spot for the people of Oldland to enjoy.

I joined the RAF at the end of 1942 and have not lived in Oldland since, however I have many, many happy memories.

REFLECTIONS OF OLDLAND COMMON
by
Ken Hicks
of Cherry Garden Lane

Ken Hicks

In those early years of the 1930's and 40's one has to remember that all the entertainment and activities were self made. Television then was no more a reality than the first man in space. Not every house in Oldland could boast of a 'wireless set' and bath nights were a major operation in front of an open fire with the last one out to empty the tub.

I still find it strange, the way the village was sub-divided into different zones. I have always found that people cling to their own part of the Common. Children from West Street, Court Road, School Lane and the 'Turn Pike' usually attended St Anne's School, where as those from upper High Street, North Street and Redfield Hill went to the British School now Redfield Edge, although of course there were exceptions to every rule.

It was because of these so-called divisions that we boys set up our own gangs and 'no-go' areas, we in Court Road being by far the better off because we had the free run of all the farm land to the south and west. This vast treck, as it seemed to us then, stretched from Poplar Farm across to 'Slippery Jim' and the old 'Pit Tump' (now the West Court Drive Area), and the whole of the Brook right to the Mill Pond. The Glenwood was another favourite with the gang, for the boys would spend hours making a dam by the old waterfall trying to make it deep enough to swim in.

The old dram road was another place where we spent hours and visits here always ended by going through the 'dark tunnel'. This was used as an air raid shelter in the early 1940s with people coming from Bristol in their hundreds during the bombing, although we never used it.

The old mill pond was a place of great beauty then, with swans, moorhens and bullrushes all around the edge. It was then a working mill, grinding meal and cattle food. To the Longwell Green side of the pond was 'Catscliff' another perfect place for tree climbing.

Our happiest hunting ground was the old quarry at the back of my father's yard. This was where, on those hot, dry summer days when the grass was full of seed, we would spend hours on our 'slide'. This consisted of a steep bank from Mr Harner's Chicken Farm to the 'old gypsy toilets'. Anyone could join in the game, in fact the more the merrier. The object of the game was to be the fastest to the bottom on a bent up toffee tray – cheating was not allowed – every one started together. I know we have stayed there until we wore the backside out of our trousers. There must be some boys that still remember this, such as John Sweet and Brian and Donald Williams.

I wonder if any of the Court Road boys remember that when we walked through the wicket gate next to Mr Lears', some of us would climb on his wall with a handfull of gravel and then try dropping them into the pigs' ears! I hope animal lovers will forgive us!

It was during my last year at St Anne's School in about 1940–41 that the war began to take on a real meaning for me. These were the days of the 'blackout' and food rationing. The raids on Bristol were very bad and at night we would sit outside the back door and watch the sky go red with the fires. There were dozens of search lights but we never saw a plane come down. The 'Homeguard' then used to drill by the village hall – it really was a 'Dads Army' and you couldn't help but laugh!

REFLECTIONS OF LIFE IN OLDLAND COMMON
by
Bill and **Margery Willmott**
formerly of High Street, Oldland Common,
now of St Barnabas House, Church Avenue,
Warmley

Story as told to David Noble in March 1993

Bill and Margery Willmott

My visit to Bill and Margery Willmott, aged 87 and 80 years respectively, was an enlightening experience as they spoke to me for over 2 hours on life in Oldland Common during their forty five years of living there.

Bill was born in Longwell Green near to Oldland Hall in March 1906. Soon after his birth the family moved to a cottage, facing Oldland Church in Court Road, Oldland Common, near to what was Lear's Bakery. He was the oldest in a family of four children with two brothers, Raymond and Alec and his sister Ivy, (Ivy Wake after her marriage.) Bill recalls an interesting story that when Ivy was a young girl a gentleman from America had called on them, making enquiries about the Willmott family. It turned out not to be their family he wanted but the other Willmott family in Oldland who lived in the High Street. However, on his return to America he sent a letter to Ivy which was addressed as follows, Miss I Willmott – At the cottage overlooking the Church on the hill, by the bridge over the brook, Oldland Common, Bristol, England, and the letter found her at the home address in Court Road!

In 1911 at the age of 5 years Bill attended the Church of England School, now St Annes'. In those days the headmaster was Mr Robert Burns and the Vicar of Oldland Church was the Reverend Cockey. There were two Junior and one Infant classes. School started at 9.00am and finished at 4.00pm and as well as the dinner hour there was a mid-morning and mid afternoon 10 minute break.

29

Bill left school at the age of 13 years and first worked at Jimmy Fry's Boot Factory opposite the Fish Shop in the High Street. From there he went to the Golden Valley Paper Mills in Bitton which was owned by the King-Smith family. After a couple of years he left and began working for Mr Jefferies the Builder in Barry Road – where Clark's Furniture Factory is today. Unfortunately at the age of 19 years he was involved in an accident and lost some fingers when using a circular saw. At 21 years Bill's father put him to train as a signwriter, working for 'Shepherds the Signwriters' and he continued in that trade as a signwriter/painter and decorator until he retired at the age of 72 years having done 51 years in the trade. Part of Bill's job was to do assignments for Mr Reg Merrett the local Funeral Director, when he used to inscribe, by hand, the brass plates for the coffins.

In the 1920s Bill said that there was only a small number of houses in Court Road. A few at the top of Court Road on the left and a group of cottages on either side at the bottom with mostly open fields and allotments in between. Bill Sweet's 'Heel' Factory making heels for shoes was also down at the bottom. Some of the cottages were referred to as 'the bunch' where the Joy, Jenkins, Long, Hicks, Lear and Fudge families lived. Mr Leach's fields were near to Mr Lear the Baker. Bill can remember both the Village Hall and the Church Hall being built in 1913 but prior to that most of 'the Common' was open fields.

Bill and Margery were married in Keynsham Church in 1934 and July 1993 saw their 59th wedding anniversary. They have four children, Shirley, Clive, Raymond and Vera, all of whom were born at their home in the High Street. Mrs Willmott recalls that the midwife was Mrs 'Granny' Jenkins of Oldland. Another well known midwife on the Common was Mrs Worlock.

They moved into their house in the High Street in the mid 1930s' and remained there for 45 years until 1980 when they moved to their present home in Church Avenue, Warmley. In those early years they paid 10 shillings (50p) per week towards their house which they described as being 'old fashioned' not having electricity or toilet and bathroom facilities. Practically, they had to start from scratch gradually modernising their home over the years as they went through life. There was never much money but they still think of it as 'the good old days'.

Bill recalled vividly that his first wage packet when he started work in the Boot Factory was 5 shillings (25p) per week and 12/6p (62½p) when he started after his training as a signwriter. It gradually increased as time went by to £2–10–0d (£2.50p), then £4–0–0d and so on.

As well as being a devoted mother to her children, Margery has nursed many of the local residents of the village during the years. She spent 28 years working as an auxillary in the Nursing Service at Snowdon Road Hospital in Fishponds, Frenchay Hospital and Anchor Nursing Home. She recalled the days when she earnt £5 per week and on receiving her wages she would buy the family a 'special treat' of strawberries, if in season, and cream.

Bill and Margery took a number of evacuee children into their home during the war and remembered many of their exploits especially when taking the children to the seaside at Weston-super-Mare by train!

Electricity came into the neighbourhood after the war in 1945 and subsequently they bought themselves an electric cooker. Later on they had a bathroom installed and during the Coronation year of 1953 they bought a television set but that meant going without a holiday that year. When interviewing Bill and Margery it was fascinating to hear of some of the events which they could recall so vividly, especially about the 'old Oldland'.

In the 1930's the first 'bus to travel from the Union Inn (now the Cherry Tree) was Bence's 'Bus which went to Warmley Hill Tram Depot Terminus in Kingswood. It was known as 'the Tin Lissie' and apparently each time the 'bus got part way up the hill some of the passengers would have to get out and push it to its destination!

Bill remembered playing as a youngster in the Dramway, on the line which was used for transporting coal from the pits at Shortwood to the barges at Londonderry Wharf on the River Avon at Keynsham. This was the line which past along the back of the houses on the left of the High Street, crossed over by Oldland Church Hall and along by Cherry Garden Lane known in those days as Bumble Lane and then on to Keynsham.

Then there were the nights on 'fire watch' during the war. Bill remembered taking his turn in the sheds opposite Oldland Council School (now Redfield Edge) and in the Corset Factory (now the Simplex Sectional Bookcases), together with Bert Mortimer, Harry Furber and Mr Palmer.

Memories of the Bitton and Oldland Flower Shows held in a field opposite Bitton Station and the shows held in Charlie Cryer's field (Park Farm) in Barry Road and then later in the 1950/60's, in the Village Hall.

The days when Sid Comley, Jim Upward and Ernie Worlock came around the village delivering milk on a horse and cart and George Edwards from High Street and Mary Smith from Redfield Hill delivering milk in their small milk churns.

The opening of Oldland Railway Station in 1935 with porters Bill Isaacs and Arthur Packer.

Bill, who was a keen follower of local sport, recalled that Oldland Football Club used to play at 'Pit Bank' near California Pit in California Road before they moved to the 'Rec' in Castle Road in the 1940's. The players changed in the Greyhound Pub in West Street and then had to walk to the ground from there. Oldland Cricket Team played their games on Jim Upward's fields at the top of Cowhorn Hill before they also moved to the 'Rec' at about the same period.

Both Bill and Margery recalled the church's Whitsun Parades around the Common in the 1950/60's. The three churches, St Anne's, Oldland Methodist and the Tabernacle used to parade following behind the Fishponds British Legion Band. Later they returned to their respective churches for tea followed by collective sports on the 'Rec'. Margery specially remembered enjoying the parents races and also dressing up her children for the fancy dress parade.

They could both recall all the various shops of the village, most of which were detailed in 'An Oldland Boy Looks Back', but with some others of particular interest. There was a bicycle shop called 'Hardings' located on the corner of School Road and Barry Road; Adams and Jefferies Funeral Undertakers used to be where Adie the butcher is in West Street today; Reg Fry's paper shop was in North Street before he moved to the High Street in the 1950's and Mr Ettle had a fish and chip shop near to the bridge in West Street between Mrs Saunders' shop and the old Greyhound Pub.

Bill and Margery said that the years in Oldland were happy although sometimes hard but the memories would always be precious and treasured because it was there that they had raised their family.

MEMORIES OF OLDLAND COMMON

Maureen Miller (Nee Williams)
formerly of North Street, now of
Forest Road, Kingswood

Maureen Miller

When David asked me to write a little piece about Oldland, my mind went back to one of my childhood memories of going 'up Englands', as we kids used to call it, the little sweet shop in North Street owned by George England and his sister Millie.

Often the door would be locked and we would rattle on the latch for one of them to come and open up for us. Sometimes though, we were able to walk straight in and I can still hear the bell to this day, clanging as we pushed open the door, whereupon either one of them would appear from the rear of the shop.

We would choose our sweets from the rows of jars standing neatly on the shelves and it always fascinated me to watch whoever was serving, wrap a piece of square paper around the index finger and proceed to make a bag in which to put either our pennyworth of sherbert or lemonade crystals.

We would then climb over the black iron gate at the side of the shop and walk along the footpath which crossed through Graham and Maude Smart's Market Garden, and also through the allotments to the 'Pick Ground'. (I never knew why it was called the 'Pick Ground'.) There we would proceed to eat the goodies which we had just bought. Sometimes it was quiet and peaceful and other times we could hear the animals in Jarrett's slaughter house nearby, crying as though they knew the fate which was in store for them.

Now of course the fields are all gone and row upon row of houses stand on 'our Pick Ground' but nothing can take away the memories I have of my halcyone days in Oldland.

Rachel Williams (Nee Martin)
formerly of High Street, Oldland Common,
now of Fairlyn Drive, Kingswood

Rachel Williams

I remember my early years of growing up in Oldland Common very well. I was born in 1943 in one of the little cottages in the High Street. When I was 6 months old my parents moved to one of the bigger houses in the High Street next door to the local fish and chip shop owned by Mr and Mrs Williams and in later years by Mr George and Nora Golding. I was the youngest of a family of 4 children born to the late Frank and Vi

Martin who were loving parents and although during these years we only had the basic essentials, they made it a very happy home. My older sisters are Grace and Joyce and my brother Anthony, known to many as 'Tony or to his close mates as 'Skinner'. My mother, however, always insisted that the family called him Anthony. On occasions I can remember doing the paper round for my brother and the route, which took about an hour, went up North Street, down Cowhorn Hill, along West Street, down Court Road and back to Reg Fry's shop in the High Street.

I can well remember my first day at Oldland Council School, now Redfield Edge, joining the infant's class and then later moving up into the juniors. Then there was the good times, playing down 'The Rec' in the school holidays, picking big bunches of cowslips in Farmer Cryer's fields and the enjoyment of playing down the old Dram Road which was a very convenient place to play.

My dad worked on the railway all his life and mum did a lot of dressmaking for many folk around the village. I can remember them coming to the house with their material for her to make curtains, dresses, suits and even bridesmaids dresses. She made my bridesmaids dresses in 1971 for my wedding in Oldland Church.

Growing up in Oldland holds many happy memories for me. They all have their own special kind of magic which I shall always treasure.

OLDLAND COMMON
as seen by
two teenagers of today
Abby Lacey and **Carrie Rivers**
both of West Court Drive

Abby and Carrie outside their school, Sir Bernard Lovell in North Street

Oldland Common of today does not support sports clubs of any kind consequently the teenagers of the village join sports clubs at their schools. The local Secondary School – Sir Bernard Lovell – is quite a popular one for the local youngsters of Oldland. It runs many sports clubs including netball, hockey, cricket, football, rugby, rounders and athletics meetings. If the pupils wish to expand on their talents then they must go further afield to other clubs such as Wick Ladies Hockey Club (whose ground has recently been moved to the all-weather pitch of the Grange Secondary School in Warmley) and Fry's Hockey Club who play on the grounds of Cadbury Ltd (Frys') in Keynsham. Further still there are clubs in areas such as Clifton and Portishead.

Leisure facilities are very limited around the Oldland area with the nearest leisure centre situated in the High Street of Keynsham. However, youth clubs and social centres can be found in Oldland itself (via the Oldland Church Hall) and outlying areas such as Longwell Green Community Centre and Cadbury Heath Social Club. The main place for teenagers in Oldland is the North Common Community Centre/Youth Club but when this is closed children in Oldland go as far as Bitton to meet friends. Usually there is a disco held every month in Oldland village based at St Anne's Church Hall. This is organised by the Church Hall Users Committee.

Young Christians growing up in Oldland have many options open to them as there are a number of churches in the vicinity. These include the United Reformed Church, St Anne's Church of England and the Methodist Church in West Street, all of which offer a variety of opportunities for their young people. As a member of St Anne's Church, the youngsters there are catered for from birth to the age of eighteen. A creche is run in the newly built Orchard Rooms along with three groups of Sunday School children aged between four and eleven years. From here, the eleven year olds go on to join Pathfinders run on Sunday evenings and then subsequently to CYFA (Church Youth Fellowship Association). At these groups the young people learn more about the Christian life and social events are organised for the members and their friends. After leaving CYFA, the young adults are welcome to join house groups.

There are many uniformed groups affiliated to the local churches including groups of Brownies, Guides, Beavers, Cubs, Scouts, Girls Brigade and Boys Brigade and all take part in evening meetings and family services.

Services are held throughout the week at various times and the Churches of Oldland invite and welcome all ages to join with them.

THE CHANGING SCENE
OF NORTH COMMON

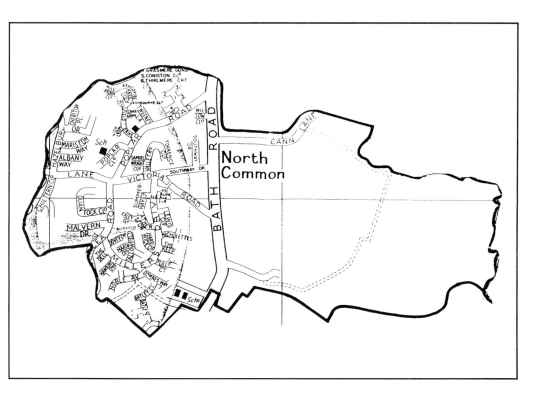

Map of North Common in the Borough of Kingswood – 1993

Situated off the main A4175 road between Oldland Common and Bridgeyate in the County of Avon is nestled the village of **NORTH COMMON**. Very little information is available about the past history of the village but records indicate that it was closely associated with the Ecclesiastical Parish and Rural District of Warmley. Hence it's postal address of 'North Common, Warmley'. It was and still is part of the Parish of Bitton. Originally, however, it is possible that it's early history relates closely with that of it's neighbouring village Oldland Common in that it was land 'north' of the 'common' fields of Oldland thus deriving the name of North Common. There is a similarity between the two 'Commons' in that North Common is also set out in a triangle of roads, namely, Poplar Road, Victoria Road and Bath Road with smaller roads leading off from these.

Certainly over the past two decades, out of the four villages featured, North Common is probably the village that has experienced the largest housing and industrial development replacing the open farmland. Extensive building programmes have taken place especially around the Poplar Road, Victoria Road, Cloverlea Road, Mill Lane, Lees Lane and the old Hardwick Farm, now known as Millers Drive, areas.

The population of the village in the earlier years of the century was around 1,000. In the 1940's and 1950's it was around 1,500 and in the early 1980's increased to around 2,700. The mid 1980's saw a significant increase to around 3,500 and the early 90's a further 200 were added to peak at around 3,700.

In the early to mid part of the century before the major housing developments brought about the 'new look' to the village, many of the residents will no doubt remember the following facilities. There were four general grocery stores, two in Bath Road, Maurice Harris and Percy Higgs and two, plus a hardware shop or 'Oil shop' on Poplar Road owned by Mr Charlie Hayman. Two Public Houses, the Railway Tavern in Poplar Road, now a private house named 'Old Tavern House' and The Hollybush on the Bath Road which was bought by Bristol United Breweries in 1897 from Daniel Sykes and Co. The Landlord today is Mr Mansell Durbin and previous Landlords/Landladies since 1910 have been , Mr W H Noble (1910), Mrs Louisa Mary Noble (1926), Mr Willie Witts (1938) and Mr Donald Bracey who took over the Pub in 1953. Since changes in the postal boundaries The Holly Bush is now addressed as part of Bridgeyate. Two churches, the Methodist Church in Poplar Road and the Brethren Salem Church built in 1871 in Cann Lane which is now closed and the premises privately owned by the Hallaran Family. Five farms (described later by Albert Lansdale) and Nowells the florist in Cann Lane. Two Coal Merchants, Howard Harris on the Bath Road and Fred Hobbs in Poplar Road. The latter is now the well known and established coach firm called Swallow Coaches. Two small garages were in operation on the Common including G S Cars owned by Mr Bernard Gray, which in later years moved to new premises in Tower Road South, Warmley and is now owned by a well known North Common resident Mr Roger Fowler. There were also three Builder's Merchants and two very thriving factories, Brain's Boot Making factory now St Stephen's Business Units in Poplar Road and Bryce White's Timber Merchants, now owned by Harcros Timber Building Supplies, on the junction of Bath Road and Victoria Road.

North Common was well represented by it's own football team 'Poplar Rovers' who played their games behind the Methodist Church on one of Farmer Busley's and later Farmers Fowler and Allen's fields.

No doubt many would be interested to know, especially local Methodists, that an entry in John Wesley's Journal for Tuesday 13th October 1761 states, *"I preached at Newgate, at Kingswood in the afternoon, and in the evening at North Common. Here a people are sprung up, as it were 'out of the earth'; most of them employed in the neighbouring brass* works. *We took a view of these next day, and one thing I learned here, the propriety of that expression from the Bible, Revelation Chapter 1 verse 15 "His feet were as a fine brass, burning in a furnace". The brightness of this cannot easily be conceived: I have seen nothing like it but clear white lightning".* Perhaps this indicates that John Wesley stayed overnight in North Common, probably with a local family!

As previously mentioned, North Common has dramatically changed over the past decade or so and although not many photographs are available of the 'old North Common' the following will reflect some of the changes which have taken place during the century.

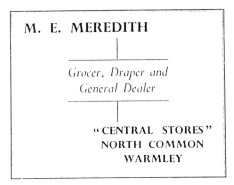
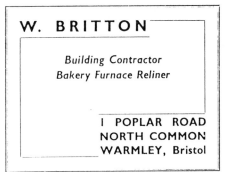
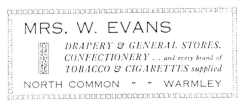
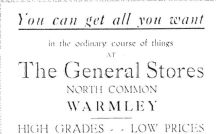

This photograph, taken in the summer of 1964, shows a steam train coming from the direction of Bath and Oldland Common and passing through North Common on it's way to Warmley and onto Temple Meads.
Photograph courtesy of Neil Burgess.

The same spot in 1993. Notice the Cycle-path and walkway and the houses on the right in the Lees Lane/Millers Drive area, formerly Mr Harold Hardwick's fields.
Photograph by the author.

'The Central Stores' on the corner of Poplar Road and Victoria Road in the 1950's. Notice the Bill board along the side of the wall indicating the films being shown that week at the Odeon Cinema in Kingswood.
Photograph supplied by Robert Lewis.

The same 'Central Stores' today in 1993

"Can I help you?" Our photograph shows Madeline Taylor (nee Lewis) giving a helping hand at Mr and Mrs Meredith's 'Central Stores', her grandparents, in 1959.
Photograph supplied by Robert Lewis, Madeline's brother.

Inside the 'Central Stores' today, slightly larger than the earlier years. Prices are somewhat different than in 1959, however service is still with a smile as Jane Campbell shows.

'Down on the farm' – Poplar Farm in Poplar Road in the early part of the century around 1905. The Busley family who owned the farm lived in the front and the Hathway family lived at the back. In later years the Fowler and Allen families took over the farm.

Warmley Church of England School in Poplar Road is now situated on the site where Poplar Farm used to be up until the late 1960's. The farm land in those days spread as far as the Mill Brook (Bottom of Mill Lane) and the 'Tumps' which were situated on the land behind the Church in the direction of Millfield Drive, Ashcombe Crescent and Ashbourne Close areas. The School moved from Church Avenue, Warmley to Poplar Road in 1974 and was opened by the Bishop of Malborough. The present Headmaster is Mr Dyson and the number of pupils in the school is 340.

These two photographs taken in the early 1950's show some of the many children of the village who used to play 'down on the farm'. In the photograph above are Frank and Rosy Allen who owned the farm at this time and also Charlie and Martha Phelps who lived in the back part of the house.
Photographs supplied by Molly Hathway of Bath Road.

Howard, Bill and Rex Nowell pictured outside 'The Bakery' (Grocery and Drapery Stores) in Bath Road in 1911. The shop in later years was owned by Maurice Harris. It closed for business in the 1960's.
Photograph supplied by Sheila Williams (nee Nowell).

Pictured outside the same building in 1993, now a private residence, are Dot Jacobs, Andrea Evans (the owner) and Mary Parker.

The Railway Tavern, situated in Poplar Road, was owned by Charlton Beers and closed it's doors as a public house in the late 1960's. The premises were built around 1820 and was thought to be originally two cottages and stables. Just about 100 yards away is 'The Holly Bush' in Bath Road, now the only public house in the village, but whose postal address is now Bridgeyate.
Photograph supplied by Dr Baldwin of Poplar Road.

The Railway Tavern as it is today. Now 101 'Old Tavern House' Poplar Road, the home of Dr Leslie and Mrs Joan Baldwin.

Situated up the lane near to the Gospel Hall and now above the area of Alec Jarretts Ltd. Meat Processing Plant is Harvey Leaze Cottage (previously known as Newports Cottage.) On the 4th July 1915 it was struck by lightning and this picture shows the extent of the damage caused.
Photograph supplied by Albert Lansdale of Victoria Road

The cottage today, nestled neatly on the hill overlooking the 'new' North Common, is the home of David and Molly Toghill. David's parents and grandparents previously lived in the cottage and can be seen in the preceeding photograph.

NORTH COMMON AND IT'S COMMUNITY

'Phoenix rising from the Ashes' – situated in Millers Drive, the 'new' and the 'old' buildings of North Common Community Centre photographed together in 1990. The Association was founded in 1971 and the temporary building was erected in 1983.
Photograph by Roger Fowler of Millers Drive.

The new building photographed in June 1993 was opened, by the then Mayor of Kingswood, Mr Les Bishop in 1991. The Centre is a hive of activity and has a regular range of events taking place for each age group every day of the week. Officers of the Centre are; Chairman – Roger Fowler, Secretary – Brenda Flay, Treasurer – Win Jackson, Booking Secretary – Carol Fowler.

Celebrations in North Common of the Coronation of our Queen, Elizabeth II on 2nd June 1953. Everyone enjoyed the party, children, parents and helpers alike.
Photograph supplied by Molly Hathway of Bath Road.

A group of those who assisted in the local organisation of the Coronation celebrations in North Common.
Photograph supplied by Molly Hathway of Bath Road.

The Poplar Rovers Football Team 1921/22 season.
Photograph supplied by Molly Hathway of Bath Road.

Poplar Rovers AFC season 1933/34
Photograph supplied by Albert Lansdale of Victoria Road.

The Homeguard Football Team season 1939/40, which consisted of many local lads from 'The Common' including; G Mortimore, G Lucas, A Taylor, W Gray, G Smart, J Lewis, E Brain, J Odey, L Cox and A Owen.
Photograph supplied by Allan Taylor formerly of North Street, Oldland Common.

Poplar Rovers Football Team season 1949/50 pictured with Grant Elston (trainer) and Dave Saunders (Mascot) are, Gordon Lines, Reg Gay, Harold Gover, John Saunders, Ken Gover, Ken Dando, Ernie Brain, Jack Lewis, George Fisher, Ken Wiltshire and Ken Mortimor
Photograph supplied by Albert Lansdale of Victoria Road.

North Common Methodist Church situated in Poplar Road was built in 1879. It has remained an active fellowship serving the community with many varied activities.

One of the many missionary meetings held in the schoolroom. Photographed in 1956 are members and friends at a meeting conducted by the Rev Phippen who had served as a missionary in India. He was the son of Mrs V Phippen, a Church member for many years who is seen in the photograph to his left.
Photograph by Malcolm E Meredith – Member of the Church for many years.

A selection of children who attended the Sunday School tea party in 1955.
Photograph by Malcolm E Meredith.

Helpers and friends pictured with the Minister Rev Francis Clutterbuck at the Sunday School tea party in 1955.
Photograph by Malcolm E Meredith.

North Common Methodist Youth Club's first 'Annual Dinner' in 1965. Photographed seated in the centre are the Minister and his wife, The Rev and Mrs Rossiter Forward.
Photograph supplied by the author.

North Common Methodist Women's Bright Hour Christmas party – 1970. The Minister, The Rev Tom Furley is seated in the centre at the back.
Photograph supplied by the author.

Annual 'Band of Hope' Whitsun Parade from North Common to Kingswood in 1958
Photograph by Malcolm E Meredith.

Young children, parents and helpers on the decorated lorry driven by Mr Howard Harris, the local Coal Merchant, during the same procession of 1958
Photograph by Malcolm E Meredith.

THE NOWELL FAMILY
REMEMBERS
NORTH COMMON

Eileen Powell and
Sheila Williams (Nee Nowell)

Among the well known families in the Cann Lane/Bath Road area of North Common is the Nowell family. Following the publication of 'An Oldland Boy Looks Back', I was delighted to receive letters from two members of this family, Mrs Sheila Williams (nee Nowell) who now lives in Fordingbridge, Hampshire, and Mrs Eileen Powell (nee Nowell), of South Molton in Devon, two sisters who were both brought up in North Common during the 1930's and 1940's.

Sheila remembers most vividly the happy times spent in the area and recalls in her letter some of the people and events of the village during that period. Eileen, in her letter, said that their father, Charles Rex Nowell who was born in 1903 and for many years had worked at Brain's Flour Mill in Tower Road , Warmley, had written a most comprehensive account of his memories of life in North Common. It is with grateful thanks to Sheila that I can include just some of her memories of the 1930/40's and with the kind permission of Eileen that I can record some of the memoirs of the late Mr Nowell.

Sheila Williams writes,
"When I was born, my parents lived in 'The Elms' Cann Lane, next door to my grand-parents. We moved to Holbrook when I was 4 years old but I regularly attended the little Gospel Hall every Sunday afternoon followed by 'bought cake' and tinned peaches for tea at gran's. Mrs Gray was our Sunday School teacher, a tall, gaunt woman with tremendous dignity.

Even though we moved to Holbrook we continued to buy our milk from Jim Upward and meat from Jim Darby of Oldland.

I went to Oldland Council School where the Headmaster was Mr Uglow, a lovely man and 'my hero'. There was an air raid shelter in the field behind the playground which we were not supposed to play in , but we did! The education seemed perfectly adequate, I don't remember being bored anyway. I cannot remember many names of friends at school except that of Brian Toghill because he put the ends of my plaits in the inkwell of his desk behind me and completely ruined my lovely red blazer – school days were happy days! The Toghill family lived at the top of the lane near the Gospel Hall.

When my dad was young, he and his brother and parents lived in the shop near to the 'Salt Box' in Bath Road, with gran's parents, the Gully's. Great grandfather Gully had gone into the pit, California Pit in Oldland, as a young boy, but somehow they still managed the shop and bakery when dad was small. They delivered the bread by pony and cart. The yeast for the bread was fetched from a brewery in Bristol. When I was a child the shop was owned by Maurice Harris. Percy Finch was next door with his cobblers shop at the rear. Apparently Percy used to go to Wales regularly to collect orders for boots which he then came back and made. Edgar Perry lived beyond the 'Salt Box' and he had a second-hand furniture shop in Stokes Croft. Many of the families living around the area of Mr Harris' shop, in Bath Road and Cann Lane, were regular worshippers at the Gospel Hall.

These are some of the people and places in my memory which will always remain with me".

NORTH COMMON
'I Can Mind The Time'
Extracts from the writings
of
Charles Rex Nowell

The Nowell family: *William Charles Nowell and Sarah Ann Nowell, pictured with their four sons in 1949, Bill, Rex (author of the text), Howard and Frank*

"In North Common, a South Gloucestershire village about a mile from the southern end of the lovely Cotswold hills, Granfer sat in his old hard back chair contentedly smoking his old cherry pipe, a constant cloud of smoke rose from behind the page he was reading, possibly the 'Christian Herald' or the 'Farm, Field and Fireside' both of which with 'The Chronicle' formed most of the reading for the family. . . . There was no Radio or Television at that time, not even a crystal set and the evenings during the week were spent reading, playing draughts and discussing local gossip. This was of course in the winter, but in the summer the evenings were spent gardening and we lads were compelled to make a reasonable effort much against our will.

Granfer took over a little shop in Bath Road, which supplied the locality with groceries, home baked bread, parafin, candles, sweets and a few lines in ladies wear. It was a general store in which I remember Woodbine cigarettes were 1½d per packet of five. . . .

It was here that I was born on March 23rd 1903, and my earliest recollection is, of being lifted out of the bath on a Friday evening and being carried by father to see Halley's Comet and being told that I would be a really old man if I lived to see it again. This stands out in my mind most vividly with my parents, grandparents and some neighbours standing in front of the old shop while I was wrapped in a large towel. It was dark and grannie said, "take the boy in Bill, he will catch his death of cold."

Brother Billy was born a year after me so very soon I was taking second place. From my little bedroom I have early recollections of a *'little window where the sun peeped in every morn.'* It looked out on to expansive meadows and woodland and also a stable for Tom, a cart shed, a pigstye, a fowlhouse which always held some noisy chickens with the early rising rooster, and a 'little house' which at that time we called the W.C. This is an abbreviation of 'water closet' and to avoid mistakes it was painted on the door in large letters.

On one occasion when we had a visit from our Perry cousins, they referred to it as the 'lavatory' and the next day Billy tried to take on this new title but he did not get it quite correct and called it the 'lavender'. Aromatically this was far from the truth and so we reverted to the old name. It could also have been termed the 'library' with more than a grain of truth because I am quite sure the 'Farm, Field and Fireside' was read with greater detail here than in the house – there was more time!

My early days at school stand out very clearly. I am told that I was four and a bit when I started. There were four or five of us new 'scholars' and we sat away from the rest fraying cloth to stuff rag dolls! What became of the dolls I do not know, but this was my earliest experience of monotonous labour without an end product. I cannot remember the dress I was in but all the boys of this age wore skirts so I suppose I was dressed the same. It was difficult to tell the boys and girls apart because all had their hair cut in the male style, no doubt for hygienic reasons.

The roads at that time were Macadam and the steel tyres of the carts ground the surface stone into a fine dust and on a fine sunny day the progress of the early motor cars could be traced by a fine cloud of dust which came up behind each car. It smothered the hedges and came into the houses and the adults could be heard to say, 'we could do with some rain to lay the dust'. When it did rain, local road men used scrapers to scrape it into heaps to be carted away. It consisted of a mixture of horse manure and grit and was sometimes used as a dressing for heavy clay land.

There were many different tradesmen calling at the cottage doors selling their wares. One man sold sand which was put on the stone flags so that when it was scuffed around it scoured the surface of the stones and made them clean. This was done on a Saturday and swept in the evening so that the floor was clean for Sunday.

Very few cottages were graced with any form of floor covering except perhaps for a corn sack which served as a rug before the fire. In contrast the 'front room' or parlour would be graced with some floor cloth, a couple of arm chairs which were probably inherited, a couch, a whatnot which carried all sorts of small ornaments and family photo's and sometimes an American organ around which they sang hymns such as 'count your many blessings name them one by one'.

Unemployment was very high in the coal and boot trades, the main avenues of employment for most of the men in the district. The only relief offered to poor families, down on their luck, was from the 'Poor Law Guardians'. Taking in washing was a common occupation for those who needed to get a few more shillings to keep the family going.

An event which gave us great pleasure and got us out of the house in which we were sometimes a bit of a nuisance, was an Easter Monday ramble. About six of us would set off over the foothills of the Cotswolds down into the lovely Golden Valley and on to the beautiful village of Upton Cheyney. Here life seemed to stand still and still does. There was a spring fountain in the wall of a garden from which many of the houses drew their water, a cold and refreshing stream of constantly running sparkling water and by the time we reached there we were just about thirsty. From here we walked up a bridle path to the Landsdown escarpment and on to the Bath racecourse where we ate our sandwiches and bought lemonade from the Star Public House.

Our old shop seemed to be a meeting place for some of the travellers who came around. For example there was old Mr Bidmead from Bath who came by train to Bitton and then foot slogged around the area selling Singer Sewing Machines on hire purchase. The war (1914 -18) put an end to his trade and after calling for a few weeks to collect his accounts he finally came to say goodbye. He was a nice old chap typical of the footsloggers of his day.

As children we took great delight in doing things, we were growing up and exploring every avenue for something new. Life seemed full of challenge and discovery and we revelled in it. . . ."

NORTH COMMON MEMORIES

by
Eileen Hembury (Nee Sheppard)
formerly of Victoria Road
now of Oldland Common

Eileen and Alan Hembury

Being a youngster in North Common was idyllic by today's standards. We spent hours playing in the streets, with very little traffic to worry about. Maybe the occasional 303 'bus from Kingswood to Cherry Garden Hill and even this ceased at 10.30pm causing many problems once we reached our teens and strayed further afield, but in the main no late nights if you lived in North Common.

There were plenty of fields to roam through. The 'tumps' at the back of Allen's farm proved a favourite, ideal for the boys. It was 'BMX' without the flash bikes with most being made up from numerous spare parts minus brakes and mudguards, even so there was some spectacular riding up and down those tumps, the rabbit holes providing extra obstacles to be avoided if you didn't want to be over the handlebars and into the brambles. Blackberry picking was another pastime, either to take home for jam and tarts or to provide some solace to an empty stomach. The more daring kid would stray into the old clay pits and sometimes swim in the water filled holes but my sister and I were banned from going anywhere near water other than the brook, and that included the new swimming pool at Warmley when it was built.

Cann Wood was another favourite place. I remember this from a girls point of view with it's abundance of bluebells, violets, primroses and wood anemones, causing me to wander for many hours. I can never remember having to be 'home for dinner'. Days out playing seemed uninterrupted and endless, where even doing nothing held something of interest even if only to watch the birds and rabbits or just kicking heads off dandelions while wandering aimlessly through the fields. The flowers we picked often brought us 3d a bunch from kindly neighbours, to be spent on blackjacks and fruit cocktails or liquorice bootlaces from Meredith's shop.

Wednesday evening, 'Band of Hope', I think the name was so apt! Mr Noble (senior) did his best to instill a sense of Christian value into what must have seemed a very ungrateful bunch of kids. I'd like to think that his efforts were not in vain. I'm sure that many of us benefitted from his efforts even though it was many years later that the 'light' dawned and his words made any sense in relation to our own personal lives.

Sunday and Sunday school were also special with the Sunday School Anniversary day in particular, with readings, recitations and songs performed in the Chapel. To me it was a day of being 'scrubbed' to excess, putting on a taffeta dress, having a ribbon in my hair and sitting with my sisters, Margaret and Kay or Molly as she was then called, looking like china dolls waiting until it was time to go to Chapel, each wearing a hand knitted cardigan with embroidered flower kindly donated by Aunty Kathy Brain.

Some of the 'learning' must have struck home because at nineteen years of age I decided to be christened along with my sister Margaret. This was on the understanding that Reverend Forward did not require me to wear anything fancy! I believe I wore a very tight fitting red tartan skirt with a white tight jumper and a white imitation leather, yes plastic, coat and 3 inch high heel shoes also in white with black stockings which had a diamond pattern on the sides! It must have been quite an event. The Chapel was full. I had never seen so many people in the little Chapel before except for Harvest Festival. All those Sunday hats and best coats, the smell of moth balls was quite overpowering! I remember that day with pride and amusement.

I missed the re-union which was held sometime ago but maybe there will be another opportunity to meet some old faces from the 50's and 60's who also have fond memories of, the little Chapel, Band of Hope, haymaking on Allen's Farm, Whitsun Parades and a host of other forgotten pastimes that made North Common such a part of our lives.

NORTH COMMON
by
Albert Lansdale
of
Victoria Road

Albert Lansdale

North Common, a small village to the north of Oldland was noted over the years for it's farms and boot-making. There were five farms in a mile radius. Bailey's Farm in Gypsy Lane now known as Cloverlea Road, Brice Farm in Victoria Road; Harold Hardwick's Farm in Lees Lane now known as Millers Drive; Busley's Farm in Poplar Road and Stump's Farm in Cann Lane. In the old days it was great to follow the mowing machine and what was known as the 'sweep' to gather in the hay and of course to have a drop of farmhouse cider!

We also had the Boot Factory in Brain's yard run by Sam Brain. His brother, namely Walter Brain owned the factory at Bridgeyate. They made all heavy army type boots and I remember my mother stitching the uppers at home. After school it was our job to clean up in those days. We had a boiler in the back kitchen to do the washing and it was heated by burning all the waste leather. Yes it was the good old days!

North Common had two pubs – The Railway Tavern and The Hollybush. The Hollybush was a family pub and it was always fund raising for the senior citizens of North Common. At Christmas they always received a present of cash. The annual 'Harvest Home', always a great success, was organised by the hard working committee led by Mr Ted Fowler, Arthur Price, Fred Condick, Jack Odey and others.

North Common was always noted for it's football team, namely 'Poplar Rovers'. They played on a field joining Busley's farm and the changing room was one of the outhouses which was cleaned up on the day of the match by the players. They had top matches playing such teams as Cadbury Heath FC and Caisley Sports. Elsie Conant was a big help to the club, washing all the shirts and of course in those days she had to do the washing in the tin bath!

NORTH COMMON
by
Marion Edwards (Nee Hathway)
formerly of Poplar Road, North Common,
now of Clyde Avenue, Keynsham

Marion and Arthur Edwards

My memories of North Common go back a long way as I lived there from 1919 to 1948 followed by a move to Downend and then to Keynsham. The years spent at North Common were very happy ones. I attended Oldland School where Mr Evans was the Headmaster and a Miss Ellis was Headmistress of the infant department. When Mr Evans retired Mr Uglow took his place. He was a younger man and we were quite fond of him.

Everyone at Poplar Road where I lived was very friendly. There were two pubs, the Railway Tavern which, when I was very young was owned by a Mr Ship and his sister and then later by Mr and Mrs Ollis. Mr Ollis worked at Filton and was killed during an air-raid in 1940. At that time I was working at Gloucester Road in Bristol and remember vividly watching the planes go over towards the Filton Aircraft factory. It was dreadful and worse still when I arrived home that night to be told that Mr Ollis had been killed in that raid. The Holly Bush on the Bath Road, still there today, was owned in those days by Marie and Bill Wicks.

Charlie Hayman had the Hardware business in Poplar Road. He would go around in his van selling oil, soap and washing powders etc. Everyone knew Charlie and then later his son Greville who helped him.

There were quite a number of cottages in Poplar Road. Lloyd Palmer lived with his mother in a small cottage opposite Mr Hayman's shop. A few newer houses were built by Hembrough Builders. Alan Gibbs lived in one with his wife Ivy and their three boys. Alan was a very good gardener, specialising in sweet peas and winning many prizes at the local Flower Shows. He died very young and then Ivy his wife took over and she did extremely well with her flowers.

On Sundays we attended the Methodist Church situated on Bridgeyate Common next to the White Hart Pub. It was and still is a lovely little Church. We had lots of fun on Sundays and at the week night meetings. There was the Guild meeting on Monday, choir practice on Tuesdays, Womens Bright Hour on Wednesday and in those days all the meetings were very well attended. The Haskins families, all of whom lived in North Common, were well represented at the Church. Herbert Haskins was the Choirmaster and Archie played the organ. My father, George Hathway, loved the 'little Church on the Common' and attended there all his life. A brass plaque is in the Church to his memory.

The Whit Tuesday parade around the village was another great and well loved event. The band used to take a break at Brain's house in Poplar Road for buns and lemonade and in later years they had their break at Stump's Farm in Cann Lane before returning to the church for tea. After tea, the band which was from Bitton and their conductor Mr Pullin, would sit outside and play whilst games were arranged for the children and a few stalls would be around. All great fun! On Whit Sunday evening we had a concert on the Common which certainly attracted the crowds.

I have only mentioned people from the bridge to the bottom of Poplar Road where it meets the Bath Road but just over the bridge was Poplar Farm where my grandparents lived. It is no longer there but I have lovely memories of playing with my cousins in the 'tump field' behind the farm and then sitting in my granny's kitchen on the old settle eating huge slices of homemade cake.

There were two shops, the first was owned by Mr Evans and the shop on the corner was owned by Mr and Mrs Meredith and their daughter May. Mr Meredith was a good photographer and because the photos he took were cheap we went to see him often to get photos to send to our boyfriends or husbands during the war.

I well remember, when I was very young, the milkman bringing the milk around daily in huge churns and then pouring it into our jugs with a one or two pint measure. Mr Downs was one of the milkmen and later on Lily Lewis took over. She lived in one of the cottages in Bridgeyate.

The Saw Mills were there in those days and still are today. Near the Saw Mills was a fish and chip shop – how we enjoyed a bag of chips on a Tuesday night going home from choir!

Bread was delivered daily. We had ours from a Mr Lacey whose bakery was at Warmley. Tuesdays were special because then we had dough cakes as well and they were very good.

We had an hourly bus service to Kingswood run by Bence Brothers of Longwell Green. Most people from Poplar Road did their shopping in Kingswood. There was also a bus service from Kingswood to Keynsham.

In those days most people grew their own vegetables and a great number kept chickens as well so that there were always fresh eggs for breakfast!

When the weather was dry, the old dram road was a quick way to walk to Warmley Station or Warmley Church but if a lot of rain had fallen then you could find yourself unable to get through the tunnel because of the mud. Many a time I can remember, having come from Bristol to Warmley Station and deciding to take the short cut home to Poplar Road through the dram tunnel only to find that part way I had to turn back and walk the long way round to Poplar Road through Bridgeyate. After a hard days work it did not go down too well!

The names of different people come to mind. The Nowell family, Mr and Mrs Nowell senior lived in Cann Lane. They grew tomatoes, cucumbers and bedding plants. Then there was Jim Fews who lived in a little cottage near the Saw Mill. He regularly attended Bridgeyate Church and no child misbehaved (although they tried!) when he was around. Clips round the ear were more free then!

I could just go on and on – there are so many people I would like to mention but I do hope this nostalgia will mean as much to the older people of North Common as it does for me.

'THROUGH THE DECADES'

CHANGES AND EVENTS IN BRITAIN 1900 – 1990

There is no doubt that this century has witnessed dramatic changes, not only in village life but throughout Britain and indeed the world.

In order to help readers reflect back on *some* of these events and changes, I have reviewed each decade separately, listing local, national and just a few international happenings. It was interesting to see what events had been happening locally in our villages whilst other events and changes had been taking place at the same time in the wider world. It is with the kind permission and assistance of the Automobile Association, Chronicle Communication Ltd., Redcliffe Press Ltd.(Bristol), Ordnance Survey and Readers Digest, together with my own personal research that this exercise has been achieved.

*   *   *

INTERESTING EVENTS OF THE DECADE 1900 – 1910

During the early Edwardian years life in Britain was generally taken at a much slower pace. These were years of peace, stability and to some degree prosperity, laying the foundation for a modern urban society. About 40% of Britons lived in towns of over 100,000 people while less than 25% lived in the rural areas.

EVENTFUL OCCASIONS

Nationally

22nd January 1901: Queen Victoria died. She was aged 81 and had reigned for 63 years.

31st May 1902: The Boer War ended. It had commenced on the 10th October 1899.

9th August 1902: Edward VII was crowned King.

1902: During this year County Councils and Urban Councils became responsible for all education in primary and secondary schools within their respective areas.

1904: During this year Rolls Royce cars were first made.

26th June 1905: The Automobile Association was founded. During this year also, driving faster than 20 mph was illegal!

July 1907: The Boy Scout Movement was formed.

1908: During this year the Olympic Games were held in London.

24th September 1908: Old Age Pensions were introduced in Britain.

The Griffin Inn, Bridgeyate, circa 1900. 'Delivery of Ale'. A drawing by Rex Whittock of Elm Bungalow, Bridgeyate. Kindly supplied by Mr. C. Hemmings of Warmley.

Locally

1901: The population in Oldland was 1,956, in North Common it was 1,000 and in Bridgeyate it was about 200.

1901: The Reverend Thomas Hireson began his ministry and eventually became the oldest Non-Conformist Minister in the Country and was known as 'The Grand old man of Oldland Common'.

1903: Golden Valley Paper Mills industry commenced in Bitton.

1904: During this year the last colliery in the Oldland Common area was closed due to flooding.

1904: The Oldland Board Mixed School was renamed as Oldland Council School and later became Redfield Edge.

1909: Bitton Council School (now 'The Meadows') was built and officially opened in 1910.

1909: California Colliery was bought by West Gloucestershire Water Company to use as a source of water.

*   *   *

INTERESTING EVENTS OF THE DECADE 1910 – 1920

The first World War fought between 1914–1918 dominated this decade. It brought with it the dislocation of British Society consequently resulting in much disruption and change.

EVENTFUL OCCASIONS

Nationally

6th May 1910: King Edward VII died.

August 1910: Talking motion pictures were demonstrated.

3rd June 1911: King George V was crowned at Westminster Abbey in London.

15th April 1912: The ship 'Titanic' sank on her maiden voyage.

4th August 1914: World War 1 was declared.

1916: During this year a loaf of bread cost 10d.

25th January 1918: Food rationing introduced in Britain.

11th November 1918: World War 1 ended. Known as the 'Great War', three quarters of a million men from Britain died for their Country.

28th December 1918: Women over 30 voted for the first time in a general election.

Locally

1910: Bridgeyate Methodist Church was 100 years old.

Anne and Clement Hicks pictured outside their cottage, 52 Court Road, Oldland Common in 1910.
Photograph supplied by Vi Walker (Nee Hicks) of Longwell Green.

1911: Oldland Tabernacle Church (United Reformed) was a 100 years old.

1912: Willsbridge Mill was built, now The Avon Wildlife Centre.

1913: Oldland Village Club and Public Hall was built.

1913: St Annes Church Hall was erected.

1913: Professor Sir Bernard Lovell, the well known astronomer, was born in Oldland Common.

4th July 1915: Harvey Leaze Cottage (Newports Cottage) in Oldland Common was struck by lightning and extensively damaged.

1916: Canon Henry Nicholson Ellacombe retired as Vicar of Bitton. His father, The Reverend Henry Thomas Ellacombe was Vicar before him and between them they served the Parish for a total of 99 years.

1918: The Bitton Recreation Club was given to the village by Mr Charles King-Smith.

1919: Bridgeyate House in Bridgeyate was 200 years old.

*   *   *

INTERESTING EVENTS OF THE DECADE 1920 – 1930

The 'Roaring Twenties' were years of a re-building process, but certainly not without experiencing its' problems. In 1926 during the general strike there was a terrible cycle of industrial decline, unemployment and social bitterness which led to the worst explosion of class conflict that Britain had ever experienced. The twenties ended with a hazy feeling of confusion and nostalgia.

EVENTFUL OCCASIONS

Nationally

1921: During this year short frocks (dresses) for women came into fashion.

26th April 1923: The Duke of York and Lady Elizabeth Bowes-Lyon were married at Westminster Abbey in London.

28th April 1923: The Great Empire Stadium staged its' first sporting occasion. Bolton beat West Ham United 2 goals to 1.

8th May 1923: Jack Hobbs the Surrey and England cricketer scored his hundredth century.

February 1924: Petrol was increased to 2 shillings (10p) a gallon.

27th January 1926: Television was first demonstrated by John Logie Baird.

4th May 1926: The first general strike in British History began after the general council of the Trades Union Congress voted to support the miners following the breakdown of their negotiations with the coal miners.

Outings to Cheddar Caves and Weston-super-Mare were always a joint event for members of North Common and Bridgeyate Methodist Churches for many years. Both photographs taken in the 1920's show those who made the respective trips in the transport of the day.
Photographs supplied by Albert Lansdale of North Common.

22nd November 1928: The first £1 and 10 shilling notes came into circulation in Britain.

Locally

1926: Oldland Common Gospel Hall was built.

1926: Bridgeyate formerly in the Wick and Abson Parish became part of the Siston Parish.

*   *   *

INTERESTING EVENTS OF THE DECADE 1930 – 1940

The 'Raging Thirties' brought with it a depression when unemployment first reached 3 million. The years leading up to the second World War (1939) were notable for scientific discovery and achievement. There was gradual economic improvement in the late 1930's, but it was war, which had been feared for sometime that eventually brought about full employment and the basis for a new social consensus.

EVENTFUL OCCASIONS

Nationally

24th April 1930: Amy Johnson completed her solo flight from Britain to Australia.

25th December 1932: King George V made the first royal Christmas Day broadcast to the Empire.

January 1933: The MCC Cricket 'Bodyline Tour' of Australia. England won the Ashes at the end of this controversial tour.

February 1933: Hoover Carpet Cleaners were sold at £4.19s.6d.

March 1934: Eggs cost between 6d and 9d per dozen.

July 1934: The Mersey Tunnel in Liverpool was opened by King George V.

6th May 1935: King George V and Queen Mary celebrated their Silver Jubilee.

3rd September 1935: Sir Malcolm Campbell set a new world land speed record with a speed of 301 m.p.h in Bluebird.

1936: During this year the school leaving age was raised from 14 to 15 years of age.

6th June 1936: Gatwick Airport in London came into operation.

August 1936: The first ever talking pictures were seen on television.

10th December 1936: The Abdication of Edward VIII took place.

February 1937: The price of petrol increased to 1/7d per gallon.

12th May 1939: The Coronation of King George VI and Queen Elizabeth took place.

3rd September 1939: War was declared on Germany by Britain and France.

Locally

1930: The present St Annes' Parish Church in Oldland Common was 100 years old.

1930: The population of Oldland Common was 2,125.

1931: The population of Bitton was 1,306.

2nd December 1935: Oldland Common Railway Station was opened.

1937: The Recreation Field (The 'Rec') was opened in Castle Road, Oldland Common.

29th May 1937: The new Sunday School building of Oldland Methodist Church was opened.

October 1937: The centenary celebrations took place of Oldland Church School which later became known as St Anne's School.

1938: The Scout Headquarters were opened in West Street, Oldland Common.

5th August 1939: An earth tremor, which caused walls in houses to vibrate, was felt at Oldland Common. People were awakened in alarm but no damage was done.

*   *   *

INTERESTING EVENTS OF THE DECADE 1940 – 1950

These years no doubt, could be considered as the 'Courageous Forties'. The war years (1939–1945) brought into relief the misery of dictatorship, the depths of depravity and the heights of courage to which man could aspire. Post War Britain promised a better deal for everyone based on consensus politics and full employment with the result that a much lighter side of life emerged.

EVENTFUL OCCASIONS

Nationally

8th January 1940: For the first time since 1918 Britain faced food rationing.

10th May 1940: Winstone Churchill became Britains' Prime Minister succeeding Neville Chamberlain. During this year 'The War Budget' introduced a purchase tax. Cigarettes cost 8d (½d on a packet).

29th January 1942: The first 'Desert Island Disc' programme was broadcast by the BBC.

8th May 1945: The War in Europe officially ended. (V.E. Day – Victory in Europe Day).

5th July 1945: The Labour Party took power in the general election.

14th August 1945: V.J. Day (Victory over Japan) Celebrations took place throughout Britain.

1st January 1947: Britains' Coal Mines became nationalised. Also during this year Britain experienced one of the worst winters ever recorded.

Winnie Lansdale, Muriel Clark and Mary Philimore of Poplar Road, North Common doing the weekly wash in the backyard in the 1940's. Brain's Boot Factory is pictured in the background.
Photograph supplied by Albert Lansdale of Victoria Road.

20th November 1947: Princess Elizabeth and Prince Philip were married.

July 1948: Freddie Mills of Britain became the World Light Heavyweight boxing champion.

29th July 1948: The Olympic Games opened in London.

12th August 1948: Morris Minor cars came off the production line.

Locally

1940: The population of Oldland was 2,200.

1940: The Dramroad Tunnel through Oldland Common was used again during World War 11 as an air raid shelter. Bunks were installed and up to 300 people would sleep there . For a short while after the war the tunnel was used as a Mushroom Farm. Now the tunnel is inhabited by bats.

1944: During this year Oldland County Primary School, now Redfield Edge, celebrated its' centenary.

1945: Dr Thomas Aubrey retired from his practice after serving for over 40 years in Bitton and the surrounding areas.

1945: The population of North Common was 1,500.

July 1947: Oldland Womens Institute was formed.

5th September 1949: The Brabazon Aircraft made its first full flight from Filton. It was the 'biggest land 'plane in the world'.

1949: The first Oldland village show was held.

The 'Homeguard' pictured outside the Village Hall during the early 1940's.
Photograph supplied by Molly Hathway of North Common.

INTERESTING EVENTS OF THE DECADE 1950 – 1960

The 'rebellious' or 'innocent' fifties no doubt marked a period of explosive change, after years of suffering and deprivation, the fifties brought about more freedom and prosperity. The fifties had arrived and Britain began to re-build and to move again. Living standards improved as never before. There was a huge expansion in the production of consumer goods and items such as televisions, cookers, fridges, record players and electric irons became common place in British homes.

Jobs became plentiful in this decade due to post war reconstruction, expanding world trade and the increase in industries. New forms of transport emerged with cars becoming more apparant on our roads. In the early part of this decade television became a nationwide phenomenon and the cinema or the 'flicks' was a regular place of entertainment for many. Was it Prime Minister Macmillan who said in the 1950's "You've never had it so good"?

The early 50's also brought about the 'Teddy Boy Era' – remember the drain pipe trousers, drapes, jackets and the crêpes. It was during the mid – latter part of this decade that the teenagers new craze was 'rock'n' roll' and many young people could be seen rocking and jiving in our dance halls, village halls and youth clubs. When the fifties began there were no 'teenagers' but at the end of the decade there were 5 million who found their identity and invented their own distinct teenage culture. Cliff Richard became Britain's number one rock and roller.

EVENTFUL OCCASIONS

Nationally

26th May 1950: Petrol rationing ended after 10 years.

7th June 1950: The BBC broadcast the first episode of 'The Archers' on the wireless.

3rd May 1951: 'The Festival of Britain' opened by King George VI.

6th February 1952: King George VI died.

16th August 1952: The Lynmouth flood disaster occurred.

2nd May 1953: 'The Matthews Final' at Wembley. Stanley Matthews won his first F.A. Cup Medal. Blackpool beat Bolton Wanderers 4 – 3.

29th May 1953: British Expedition conquers Everest. Edmund Hillary and Sherpa Tensing reached the summit of Everest.

2nd June 1953: The Coronation of our present Queen, Queen Elizabeth II at Westminster Abbey.

September 1953: Stiletto heels became the latest footwear for women.

20th October 1953: The Ford Popular became the world's cheapest four cylinder car priced at £390 (including tax).

1954: During this year Dr. Billy Graham the American Evangelist drew large crowds to Harringay Arena in London.

6th May 1954: Roger Bannister became the first man to run a mile in under four minutes.

3rd July 1954: Food rationing in Britain finally ended.

13th July 1955: Ruth Ellis became the last woman to be hanged in Britain.

October 1956: The Suez Canal Crisis began.

1st November 1956: The first premium bonds went on sale in Britain.

1957: The 'Rock and Roll' era took off in Britain.

6th February 1958: Members of the Manchester United Football team, the 'Busby Babes', were killed in an air crash at Munich Airport.

5th December 1958: The first stretch of motorway in Britain, the 8 mile Preston By-Pass in Lancashire, was opened by Prime Minister Harold MacMillan.

Locally

1951: During this year Oldland Common Secondary Modern School was opened and Mr R. Evans was appointed as headmaster.

1952: Mr Walter Jefferies of West Street, Oldland Common, retired as Postmaster for the district having held the post for over 40 years.

12th July 1952: The old police station in High Street, Oldland Common, moved to new premises in West Street next to the village hall.

12th February 1953: Emma Hunt of Oldland Common, South Gloucestershire's oldest resident, died at 101 years of age.

February 1954: The Britannia on a routine flight crash landed in the Severnside mud.

1955: The first piece of land became available for sale – Mr Leach's paddock. This was the beginning of the West Court Estate in Oldland Common.

14th October 1955: The death of The Reverend Thomas Hireson in Oldland Common, at the age of 97 years.

1955: The Rising Sun Public House in Bitton closed as a licensed premises.

1956: During this year the building of the Oaklands Estate, in Oldland Common, was commenced.

August 1956: There was an outbreak of Foot and Mouth Disease on Weston Court Farm in Oldland Common.

September 1956: The new Secondary Modern School for Girls in North Street, Oldland Common, was officially opened.

1st May 1957: Bristol's Lulsgate Airport was officially opened by the Duchess of Kent.

26th September 1957: Lewis' new super store opened in the Horsefair in Bristol

3rd July 1958: The Greyhound Public House, in Oldland Common, closed its doors for the last time.

1958: The population of Oldland Common was 2,750.

1959: Bitton Methodist Church in Mill Lane celebrated its centenary year.

INTERESTING EVENTS OF THE DECADE 1960 – 1970

Undoubtedly this was the decade of the 'Swinging Sixties'. By the mid 1960's life for the British became distinctly better as people became more affluent. Homes were better furnished, families increasingly had cars and more people could manage a summer holiday abroad in the sun of Italy, Spain or France. The 'Beatles' – 'The Fab four from Liverpool' – had a great impact on the teenagers with their pop music. Generally, there appeared to be much more evidence of young people's support for their favourite rock groups and super sporting, rock and film star heroes. Pop music became a major industry and we saw a change in youth culture with the rise of 'Mods and Rockers', 'Hippies' and 'Punks'. It was the era of Kennedy, the mini skirt, Flower Power and student protests. England's victory over West Germany in the 1966 World Cup at the Wembley Stadium brought a feeling of great national pride. Towards the end of the 60's unemployment began to increase with the value of the £ falling by half.

EVENTFUL OCCASIONS:

Nationally:

19th September 1960: 344 tickets were issued in Central London on the first day of parking tickets and traffic wardens.

31st December 1960: This was the last day for call up to the National Service in the United Kingdom.

12th April 1961: *International news was made when Soviet Astronaut Yuri Gagarin made the first manned space flight.

6th May 1961: Tottenham Hotspur became the first football team this century to achieve the F.A. Cup and League double.

4th June 1961: Cigarettes increased by a half-penny to 1/9d for ten.

20th July 1962: The World's first passenger hovercraft service opened across the estuary of the River Dee between Rhyl and Wallasey.

8th August 1963: The Great Train Robbery took place. The gang escaped with mailbags containing £2.6 million.

22nd November 1963: *International news – The President of the United States of America, John F. Kennedy was assassinated in Dallas Texas.

January 1964: Government figures showed the average weekly wage was £16.14s.11d

16th October 1964: Labour won the general election and thus came to power again after 13 years of Tory rule. Harold Wilson became the Prime Minister.

24th January 1965: The great British Statesman, Sir Winston Churchill died aged 90 years.

16th February 1965: Following Doctor Beeching's report, British Rail network was reduced by half.

30th July 1965: Figures showed that ITV's 'Coronation Street', was the most popular weekly T.V. programme.

30th July 1966: England defeated West Germany 4 – 2, to win Soccers World Cup for the first time.

21st October 1966: The Aberfan disaster near Merthyl Tydfil, South Wales occured killing 116 children and 28 adults when a coal tip collapsed on top of the school.

28th May 1967: The lone Yatchsman Sir Francis Chichester ended his epic 28,500 mile voyage around the world at Plymouth.

29th September 1967: Cunard Liner Queen Elizabeth II was launched at Clydebank.

November 1967: The worst financial crisis for nearly 20 years ended with a devaluation of the pound.

3rd December 1967: *International news – The World's first human heart transplant was successfully carried out in Cape Town, South Africa, by Professor Christian Barnard.

29th May 1968: Manchester United won the European Cup beating Benfica 4 – 1 at Wembley.

1969: During this year Britain discovered oil reserves in the North Sea. It also marked the deployment of British troops to Northern Ireland.

1st July 1969: The formal investiture of the Prince of Wales took place at Carnarvon Castle.

21st July 1969: *International news – American astronaut Neil Armstrong became the first man to set foot on the moon.

Locally:

1961: Oldland Tabernacle Church celebrated it's 150th Anniversary.

1963: During the terrible winter of this year water lorries brought supplies to Oldland Bottom.

1963: The demolition of Bence's shop in Bridgeyate to make way for the crossroads reorganisation.

1966: The remaining land of Mr Leach's poultry farm in Oldland Common was sold and used for building. These were the 'Federated Homes'.

6th March 1966: The last passenger train for the Midland Railway ran between Bristol and Bath. The Oldland Common and Bitton Stations were subsequently closed.

8th September 1966: The Severn Bridge was officially opened by Her Majesty Queen Elizabeth II at a cost of 8 million pounds.

1967: The terraced houses, no's 154 – 162 High Street, Bitton were 200 years old.

10th July 1968: Severe floods in the area caused extreme damage and disruption.

September 1968: Both the Secondary Schools in Oldland Common were jointly re-named The Sir Bernard Lovell School for Boys and Girls.

A surprise catch in Bitton. A fish caught in the flooded High Street is displayed by Geoffrey Bush and Nigel Gay, during the terrible floods of 1968.
Photograph courtesy of Bristol Observer.

INTERESTING EVENTS OF THE DECADE 1970 – 1980

THE UNCERTAIN 70's. Despite the prosperity achieved since the world war, it could not be sustained and by the mid 70's inflation had reached 27%. There was a noticeable decline in the production of goods and unemployment reached levels similar to those of the 1930's.

Decimalisation was introduced in 1971 and caused considerable confusion among the British public especially the elderly. A national miners strike was called in 1972 and two years later, following another miners strike, a general election gave a small majority to Labour.

The 1970's brought Britain into its own major development with the North Sea oil reserves and North Sea natural gas.

Although average earnings rose between 1973 and 1983, nearly 5 million households continued to live in overcrowded conditions. 5% of households, mostly privately rented, shared such basic amenities as, hot water, bath and outside toilet.

Between 1973 and the early 80's the proportion of pupils and students in full time education showed an increase.

EVENTFUL OCCASIONS

Nationally

1st January 1970: The Age of Majority was lowered from 21 years to 18 years in Britain.

16th March 1970: The New English Bible sold one million in a day.

2nd January 1971: 66 people were killed at a football match at Ibrox Park in Glasgow.

15th February 1971: After centuries of dealing in pounds, shillings and pence Britain changed to decimal currency.

July 1971: *International news – The first heart and lung transplant was performed by Professor Christian Barnard.

1972: Pocket calculators appeared on the market for the first time.

28th May 1972: The Duke of Windsor, formerly King Edward VIII died at the age of 77 years.

1st January 1973: Britain became members of the European Common Market.

1st April 1973: Value Added Tax (V.A.T) came into effect in Britain.

January 1974: Britain went onto a three day working week.

24th April 1975: Unemployment hit the one million mark.

June 1975: The first oil was extracted from the North Sea.

21st June 1975: West Indies won cricket's first World Cup by beating the Australians by 17 runs at Lords.

1976: The hottest summer so far this century. Sports Minister Mr Dennis Howell was created 'Minister of Drought'.

1977: This year was the Queen's Jubilee Year and many street parties took place throughout the Country to celebrate the occasion.

A happy Nona Smailes and former HTV Personality Alan Taylor enjoying themselves at the first Oldland Village Club Gymkhana and Show held at Weston Court Farm in 1970.
Photograph supplied by Maureen Hemings formerly of High Street, now of Wick.

1st July 1977: This year was Wimbledon's Tennis Centenary year. Britain's Virginia Wade won the Ladies' Championship title.

3rd April 1978: The BBC began regular broadcasts from the House of Commons.

26th July 1978: The World's first 'test tube' baby was born at the District General Hospital in Oldham.

3rd May 1979: Margaret Thatcher became Britain's first woman Prime Minister.

27th August 1979: Earl Mountbatten was killed on his boat in Eire by an I.R.A. bomb.

Locally

5th July 1970: S.S. Great Britain returned to Bristol from the Falkland Islands.

July 1970: Oldland Common Village Club held it's first Gymkhana and Show at Weston Court Farm.

1971: North Common Community Association was founded.

1971: Oldland Methodist Church celebrated it's Centenary year.

1972: Avon Valley Railway was founded.

29th July 1973: The 'Brethren' meeting room in Cloverlea Road, Oldland Common, closed it's doors as a place of worship.

November 1973: The Oldland Horticultural Society was formed and the first show was held in August 1974.

1974: Local Government re-organisation took Oldland, North Common, Bridgeyate and Bitton out of South Gloucestershire and into Avon.

1974: Warmley Church of England Primary School moved from Church Avenue, Warmley, to new premises in Poplar Road, North Common.

April 1976: Bristol City Football Club won promotion to the First Division of the Football League after 65 years. City's manager was Alan Dicks and the team was captained by Geoff Merrick.

1979: North Common Methodist Church celebrated it's Centenary Year.

*　　　　　　*　　　　　　*

INTERESTING EVENTS OF THE DECADE 1980 – 1990

THE ENTERPRISING 80's. The 1980's saw widening gaps between rich and poor, employed and unemployed and prospering and depressed regions. Living standards, education and work opportunities during this time, very much depended on where people lived and on their class and ethnic background. For those in employment in the 80's it brought affluence, especially in the southern areas of the Country where computer and electronic industries had grown. Technology created a new range of consumer goods. Home computers, video – tape recorders, personal cassette – radios and cable TV became increasingly common in British homes. Consumer spending in the 80's also reflected a growing public concern with diet, health and fitness in general. In particular the interest in jogging, aerobics and health foods grew.

EVENTFUL OCCASIONS

Nationally

1980: Half of Britain's married women went out to work – the highest proportion in any of the Common Market Countries.

5th May 1980: SAS men stormed the Iranian Embassy in London to free hostages.

July 1980: Bjorn Borg won his fifth Wimbledon Tennis final.

8th December 1980: Ex Beatle, John Lennon was shot dead in New York.

29th July 1981: The wedding of Prince Charles and Lady Diana Spencer took place in St.Paul's Cathedral.

26th January 1982: Unemployment in Britain was above 3 million for the first time since the 1930's.

2nd April 1982: Argentina invaded the Falkland Islands. Our Task Force set sail for the South Atlantic on April 5th and the Argentinian forces surrendered on 14th June 1982.

28th May 1982: John Paul II arrived in Britain for the first Papal visit since 1531.

1982: Home computers became increasingly common. This was the start of the computer era.

20th July 1982: IRA bombs killed soldiers and horses in Hyde Park and Regents Park in London.

2nd October 1983: Neil Kinnock became leader of the Labour Party.

14th June 1984: A change in the divorce laws enabled couples to end a marriage after one year instead of three.

12th October 1984: IRA bomb blasted the Tory Party Conference at the Grand Hotel in Brighton.

3rd March 1985: The year long miners strike ended in Britain.

11th May 1985: More than 40 soccer fans died in a fire at Bradford City Football Club.

6th July 1988: Piper Alpha oil rig in the North Sea exploded killing 66 people.

12th December 1988: 36 people died and more than a hundred were injured in the Clapham Junction train crash. This was Britain's worst railway disaster for more than 20 years.

22nd December 1988: A Pan American jumbo jet crashed onto the town of Lockerbie in the Scottish Borders. 300 people died in Britain's worst air disaster.

April 1989: The Hillsborough Football Disaster in Sheffield. 95 Liverpool fans died when they were crushed during an FA cup match against Nottingham Forest.

9th November 1989: *Internationally – East German border points were opened followed by the demolition of the Berlin Wall.

Locally

1980: Rose Cottage in West Street, Oldland Common, the birthplace of Sir Bernard Lovell, was 200 years old.

1980: St Anne's Parish Church, Oldland Common, celebrated it's 150th Anniversary.

September 1980: Cherry Garden Primary School was opened.

1982: The Oldland United Choir was formed under the leadership of Brenda Andrews.

1983: North Common Community Centre (Temporary building) was opened by The Reverend Hilary Cooke. (The permanent building was opened in 1991 by Councillor Les Bishop)

1985: Bridgeyate Methodist Church celebrated it's 175th Anniversary.

1986: Oldland United Reformed Church celebrated it's 175th Anniversary.

1986: The population of North Common increased dramatically to around 3,500 due to extensive building projects within the area during the early to mid '80s. The population in Oldland was 3,200, in Bridgeyate it was around 530 and in Bitton it was 1,864.

1987: St Anne's School, Oldland Common, celebrated it's 150th Anniversary.

Cherry Garden Primary School (year 5) photographed with their teacher Miss Wood. (1992 – 1993)
Photograph by John Channing, Pickwick Portraits of Keynsham.

FORWARD INTO THE 1990's

A new decade, new resolutions and new hopes. Each decade is history in the making. What will this decade bring? It started with the resignation of Britain's first woman Premier, Margaret Thatcher. What other eventful occasions will occur in the next ten years? As time goes by we are making history and memories and we can each play our part to make those memories good.

AROUND AND ABOUT
BRIDGEYATE

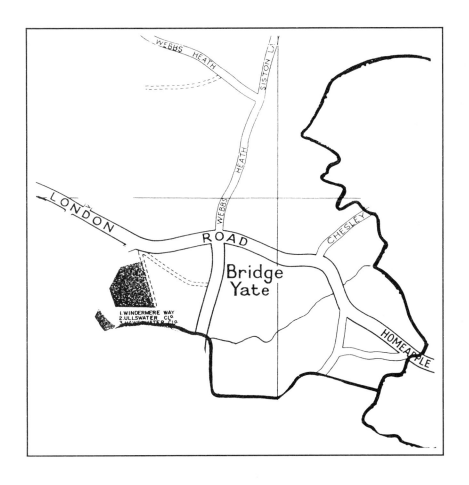

Map of Bridgeyate in the Borough of Kingswood – 1993

It is probably most unlikely, when browsing through the local history shelves in the library or local bookshop, that you will find a book solely about the locality of **BRIDGEYATE.** This comparatively small 'through' village situated on the A420 London Road between Warmley and Wick certainly has an identity of it's own. I write 'through' village with respect, for on most days of the week a continuous stream of traffic can be seen passing 'through' between Bristol and Chippenham.

The name Bridgeyate or 'Bridge Gate', formerly a small hamlet, may be derived from one of two sources. It could either have come from the gate near St Bridget's well, which is opposite Bridgeyate House in the direction of Wick, or it may refer to a gate, located on the edge of the Kingswood Forest adjoining fields known as 'Breeches' and therefore known as 'Breeches Gate'. Bridgeyate House itself is a most interesting building. A small Georgian house built in 1719 and further extended in Victorian times.

Up until 1926 Bridgeyate was part of the Wick and Abson Parish and Bridgeyate crossroads and Toll house marked the Wick boundary until that time. It is now part of the Parish of Siston. The population of Bridgeyate today is around 560 residents.

The focal point of Bridgeyate was the road junction which used to be a turnpike crossroads. Many locals will no doubt remember 'Bence's' shop on the left hand corner of the junction coming from Wick and leading onto 'the Common'. Behind the shop and at the back of Bence's garden was a slaughter house and further beyond across the 'Common' was situated Bridgeyate Cricket Club Pavilion. Bridgeyate had a good cricket team during the 1930's to 50's and they played regular fixtures on the Common.

On the opposite side of the junction towards Warmley there was a garage which used to be owned by Mr Ron Wakefield. Today it is the Bridgeyate Service Station. Across the road, directly opposite the garage, was and still is, one of the two Public Houses in the village. 'The Griffin' Public House was built in the early 18th Century as a farmhouse. Inside the pub can be seen the references to various claims to royal land. The Pub was purchased by Bristol United Breweries in 1897. Mr Martyn Merckel is the present landlord. Many will remember a popular Wednesday Market which was held at the rear of the Pub on the site of the existing car park. On the land beyond this, the North Rangers Cycle Speedway Club met regularly every Saturday evening in the early 1950's. Before moving to the land behind 'The Griffin', the 'Rangers' or 'Skid Kids' had previously met on Bridgeyate Common. The other popular Pub situated along the road towards Wick is 'The White Harte' now under the management of Mr Derek Turner. Pete and Maureen Wiltshire were once the well known Landlord and Landlady of the Pub and Pete's parents before them. (The Holly Bush of North Common, since the postal changes is now addressed as Bridgeyate).

Bridgeyate's only Church, Bridgeyate Methodist, 'the Chapel on the Common' is situated immediately right of the White Harte in the Wick direction. This Church is the oldest Methodist Church in the Kingswood Methodist Circuit and was built in 1810. The Church celebrated it's 175th anniversary in 1985 and a booklet written by Mr I H Dearnley M.B.E. to commemorate the occasion states, *"John Wesley and his fellow Methodists from Kingswood School are reputed to have preached many times on Bridgeyate Common; local family traditions are more specific adding that his horse was tethered to the old chestnut tree."* Previous to 1810 worshippers had gathered in local houses and it was on 10th of February 1810 when it was announced that John Trubody would let them have a small plot of land above the Common, on which to build a Chapel. The booklet explains further, *"John Trubody, 'Yeoman of the Parish of Wick and Abson', signed a one year lease on 23rd March 1810, at a peppercorn rent. A full conveyance was signed the next day of "all that plot of ground, containing six perches of a close of ground called "PROWT CLOSE", belonging to a dwelling house called The White Hart Inn and situate at BREACH*

YATE . . . adjoining the Common called Breach Yate Common . . . for and in consideration of the sum of FIVE SHILLINGS." Some of the family names listed in the booklet who were associated with the Church are Trubody, Sevier, Brain, Hathway, Lucas, Paget, Jelf, Kembrey, Dovey, Lansdale, Haskins, Fews, Peacock, Jarrett, Ashley, Wilmot, Potter, Parker, Johnson, Brewer, Jefferies, Hicks, Summerill, Woodington and Marks.

Surrounding the open Common land are various houses and buildings and directly opposite the Church is Elm Farm. Further across the Common towards North Common on the Bath Road is nestled Manor Farm. Many residents will no doubt remember Rear Admiral and Mrs Hughes-Onslow and the Messenger family who occupied the farm during the early to mid century. The owners of this property were recognised as Lord and Lady of the Manor. Can residents also remember the Jersey cows and 'the bull' and the very delicious cream which could be obtained from the farm!? The owners today are Mr and Mrs Isar.

In this area were also the small shop owned by Mrs Jefferies and Bendry's Sawmills Timber Merchants and on the opposite side of the road was Walter Brain and Son Ltd, the Boot Manufacturers, now owned by McBraida plc.

Taking the road in the other direction towards Homeapple Hill and Wick, many will remember the Builders' Merchants, J A Trubody who occupied those premises for many years. It is now owned by West Coast Contracts.

Across the junction towards Webbs Heath, which I intend to cover in more detail in a future publication, there are more interesting buildings. Particularly around Webbs Heath Common are the old miners cottages and Siston Parish National School which was built in the 1820's. Further along on the left hand side is Webbs Heath Farmhouse a 16th century building, built around 1530 and substantially altered and restored in the 17th century.

Although Bridgeyate is a 'scattered village' due to the central cross roads and the main road running through, it still presents as a village with history and character and the villagers create a friendly atmosphere.

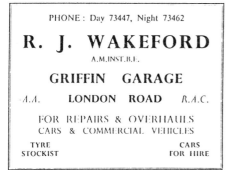
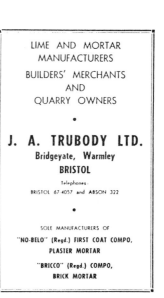

'At The Cross Roads.' An ariel view of Bridgeyate in 1989 depicting 'The Griffin Inn' on the near corner, opposite is the Bridgeyate Service Station and to the left on the London Road towards Wick can be seen 'The White Harte'
Photograph supplied by Mrs Sandra Tranter of Tennis Court Road, Kingswood.

London Road, Bridgeyate in the early 1900's photographed from the approach road into the village coming from Warmley. The population of Bridgeyate around this time was about 220.
Photograph from the M J Tozer Collection.

London Road today. Long gone are the horse and carts as a form of transport. A steady flow of traffic can be seen passing through between Bristol and Chippenham. The population of Bridgeyate today is around 560.

A drawing, by Rex Whittock of Elm Bungalow, Bridgeyate, showing Bence's shop as it was, situated on the junction of The London Road and Bath Road (on the Wick side). It sold a variety of confectionary goods and was demolished in 1963 to make way for the crossroad re-organisation.

The crossroads or double roundabout as it is today with the open space where Bence's shop once stood.
Photograph by the author.

The Griffin Inn on the cross roads in the centre of Bridgeyate was a public house owned by Bristol United Beers. This photograph was taken in the early 1940's just after it had been reconstructed and given a face lift.
Photograph courtesy of Martyn Merckel the present Landlord.

'The Griffin' today. A warm and friendly Pub and restaurant

'The White Hart' pictured in the early 1950's.
Photograph supplied by Peter and Maureen Wiltshire, former Landlord and Landlady of the Pub.

'The White Harte' today. Photograph taken in the summer of 1993. Many admire the beautiful hanging baskets and tubs of flowers outside this friendly Pub.

"The Chapel on the Common".

1739 onwards:

John Wesley and fellow reformers are reputed to have pioneered by preaching on Bridgeyate Common. (House meetings also preceded the 1810 Chapel.)

Known as 'The Chapel on the Common', this is the oldest Methodist Church in the Kingswood Circuit having been built in 1810.

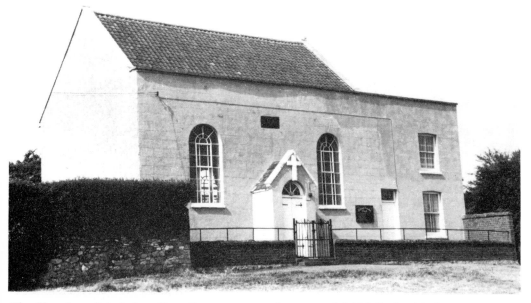

The Church as it is today. Over the years many have served faithfully in this fellowship which overlooks Bridgeyate Common.

Many 'get togethers' of Bridgeyate and North Common Methodist Churches have taken place over the years. These two photographs show members and friends at Christmas celebrations in the early 1960's.
Photographs supplied by Molly Hathway of Bath Road.

'Cricket on the Common.' The Bridgeyate Cricket Team taken in the 1920's.
Photograph supplied by Albert Lansdale of North Common.

'The opening batsman is ready to take strike!' The cricket pitch was situated 'on the Common' not far from The White Harte and the Methodist Church pictured in the background just beyond the London Road.
Photograph supplied by Peter Wiltshire of 'The Cottage' White Harte, Bridgeyate.

A close up of Bridgeyate House built in 1719 situated on the right hand side of the London Road in the direction of Wick.

Another view of Bridgeyate House with an extension to the left added in Victorian times. It is now the home of Mr and Mrs J H Wyatt.

'LIFE IN BRIDGEYATE'
by
Peter and **Maureen Wiltshire**
of
'The Cottage' White Harte, Bridgeyate

As told to Dave Noble in September 1993

Peter and Maureen Wiltshire

Pete Wiltshire has lived in Bridgeyate all his life. He was born in 1931 at the 'Yew Trees' some 100 yards or so away from the White Harte Public House of which his parents, Albert and May became Landlord and Landlady in 1933. Albert and May ran the pub together until 1948 when Albert died and May continued on her own until 1960 when Pete and Maureen took over retaining the tenancy of the premises until 1988.

The Owners of the Pub in 1900 was Ashton Gate Breweries when the Landlords were the Bristow family and later when it was sold to Georges the Seaton family took over. It is now owned by Courages Ltd. The deeds of the Pub go back to 1825 but the premises were built some years earlier. Minor building alterations have taken place over the years but major work was done in 1962 and more recently in 1989 when a complete refurbishment of the premises took place.

Pete can remember back in the 1940's when beer was rationed and his father was only allowed 7 bottles of whisky a month. There were times when beer was not available at all and the Pub was only open 3 days a week.

At the age of 5 years Pete attended Warmley Church School and remembers that there were 5 classes and 5 teachers at the school. Progressing on from there he then attended Kingswood Grammar School (now Kingsfield) leaving at the age of 16 years to commence employment with Alec Gifford of Blue Lodge, Abson, working on the farm for the next 14 years.

1959 saw the marriage of Pete and Maureen in Warmley Church and a year later they took over the full responsibility of running the White Harte from Pete's mum. Maureen (nee Gay) was born in nearby Webbs Heath and later moved to Cann Lane, North Common. She also attended Warmley Church School and then went on to Oldland Secondary Modern School. As Landlord and Landlady of the Pub both Pete and Maureen have many rich and interesting memories over the past four or five decades of Bridgeyate and it's people and between them shared some of these with me. Following retirement they moved to the cottage directly behind the Pub and are still there today. The cottage had been owned by the Wiltshire family for many years.

Basically Bridgeyate has seen very little change over the years. Since the demolition of Bence's shop on the corner of the cross roads in the early 1960's only one bungalow has been built. However, since recent postal boundary changes a section of nearby North Common is now addressed as Bridgeyate thereby seemingly increasing the population of the village.

Many of the tall oak and elm trees were cut down from around the Common in the 1960's and the one time busy Wednesday Cattle Market, situated behind the Griffin Public House, closed in the early 1970's. This market used to be the highlight of the week in Bridgeyate with farmers coming from miles around to sell and buy their stock. It also gave the opportunity for locals to buy other available produce. Bence's shop also benefitted from the market by providing teas for the farmers. Ron Wakefield's garage was at one time situated next to the Griffin Pub until he moved to new premises on the opposite side of the road where Bridgeyate Service Station is today.

Maureen remembered that in the 1950's on almost every Saturday evening in the summer the North Rangers Cycle Speedway Club met behind the Griffin on a piece of land near to the cattle market. She also remembers the butcher Jim Darby from Oldland Common regularly delivering meat around the area.

The 'Common' used to be a hive of activity up until the 1960's. Cricket was played regularly on the Common by Bridgeyate Cricket Team until the 1950's and many cars could be seen parked either on the grass or on the roadside with people watching the progress of the game. The Cricket Club later moved their pavilion and played their matches at a ground in Siston. Well known local cricketers in the team during those days were Archie Bolton and George Kembrey.

Every Whitsun, members and friends of Bridgeyate Chapel used to parade around the district and after tea met on the Common to listen to the band. In the earlier years it was the Bitton Band who entertained but in the 1950's and 1960's the Marshfield Town Band featured regularly. Other events were organised by the Church especially activities for the children. Pete can vividly remember Mrs Brewer selling cockles underneath the Elm trees; coconut shies; pony and cart rides and sports for the children.

It is also reputed that John Wesley the founder of Methodism once preached on the Common in the mid 18th century.

The local farmers had grazing rights on the Common and cows could be seen wandering and grazing across the wide open green pastureland of the Common. Surprisingly they never caused problems for the passing traffic although many a motorist in his parked car has been confronted with a cow's head peering through the car window! It was about 20 years ago that the last cows were seen grazing on the Common and these belonged to Mrs Price who owned one of the nearby farms. Interesting information about the rights of the Common was that all the farms registered in the area had 'Common' rights and grazing on the land and it was the responsibility of the Lord and Lady of the Manor, (Admiral and Mrs Onslow at that time), to collect a shilling (5p) a year from all the local farmers in order to retain their rights. Apparently Mrs Onslow also owned 6 Jersey cows and Pete says that she made the best ice-cream for miles around!

As long standing residents of the village Pete and Maureen have been associated with or can recall many of the family names and characters of Bridgeyate. Perhaps among the most familiar of names to spring to mind are Trubody, Robins, Bence, Onslow, Whitchurch, Jefferies, Brain and Wiltshire but other well known names of families who contributed much to village life were Robinson, Cook, Bryant, Davies, Price, Cooper, Seaton, Jay, Lucas, Horton, Kembrey, Bolton, Stedman, Wyatt, Downs, Cox, Cross, Lewis, Iles, Paget, Drewe and Brewer. Some of the well known characters of the village over the years have been Ron Wakefield the garage owner, Fred Whitchurch who loved to watch the cows grazing on the Common, Henry Trubody the well known local Builders Merchants, Hubert Hallows, and Rex Whittock of Elm Bungalow who has lived in the village for over 20 years and done sterling work within the community.

Pete and Maureen said that the years in Bridgeyate have been happy ones and they hope that by sharing just some thoughts about Bridgeyate and it's people will bring back memories to other residents past and present.

BITTON
YESTERDAY AND TODAY

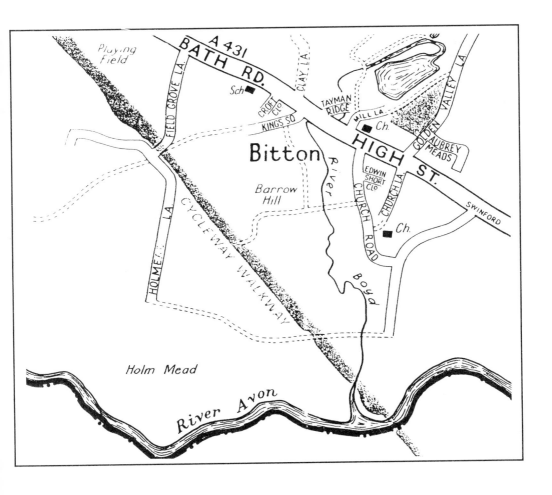

MAP OF BITTON IN THE BOROUGH OF KINGSWOOD – 1993

Apart from it's natural beauty the village of **BITTON** and it's buildings are well endowed with local history. The Kelly's directory of Gloucestershire 1906 states *"that Bitton is an extensive Parish in a fertile valley on the London Road. It is divided from Somerset on the south by the River Avon, 6 miles east-by-south from Bristol and 6 miles west from Bath and 112 miles from London. The soil is loamy, subsoil, rock and coal. The chief crops are wheat, barley and oats, and about one half of the land is in pasture. The 'Boyd Brook' runs through the village."*

In the local government re-organisation of 1974 Bitton then became part of the new County of Avon. The first recording of Bitton is in the Domesday Book of 1086, which implies there was a manor there at that time. Newton, Fitz-Harding and Berkeley were names of some of the Lord's of the Manor of Bitton. The modern spelling of the village name first occured in 1248, but a spelling of 'Boyton' was found in 1275. The name 'Bitton' means 'town or village on the River Boyd', coming from the Saxon word 'tun' meaning 'farmstead' or 'village' and a corruption of the name 'Boyd'.

The earliest published records available of the population of the Ecclesiastical Parish of Bitton was in 1931 when it recorded 1,306 residents. Estimated figures published by Avon County Council for Kingswood Borough in 1981 was 1,958, in 1986 it was 1,864 and in the early 90's 1,800.

The main road leading into Bitton Village from the direction of Hanham and Willsbridge is the A431 Bath Road which was built by the Romans and was known as the 'Via-Julia' Road.

Bitton is without doubt favoured with possessing many historical buildings. Coming from the direction of Willsbridge on the right hand side is King's Square where there are a number of picturesque mid 19th century cottages and at the top of the square is nestled Hunter's Hall, built in 1833 of gothic styled architecture. After crossing over the River Boyd the Bath Road leads into High Street – 'the hub of the village'. On the left hand side are the village shops including the village post office. Directly opposite the post office is Bitton's only Public House – The White Hart, previously a brew house of 18th century origins. There used to be another Pub called, 'The Rising Sun' which closed it's doors as a licensed premises in 1955. The Spar shop in the High Street was also previously a licensed premises known as The Kings Arms and was owned by Bristol United Breweries. Numbers 154 to 162 High Street are interesting terraced buildings, built in 1767. Two of the cottages to the left were once the village constable's house and the 'lock up', whilst the others served as a poor house for the village and later on was a pin making factory.

No visitor to Bitton should miss the opportunity of visiting St Mary's Church and it's surrounds. Church Road and Church Lane are without doubt Bitton's pathway into history. St Mary's Church dates back to at least the Norman period, with some evidence of Roman and earlier buildings on the site. The north Lady Chapel, named St Catherine, dates from 1299 and was erected by Thomas de Buttun (or Bitton), Bishop of Exeter. A tower and chancel to the west was built in 1377. Next to the Church is The Grange, the most historic house in Bitton. It was built in the 12th century and converted to a hall house in the middle ages with remodelling and rebuilding taking place in the 17th and 18th century. In 1742 William Seymour murdered his brother Berkeley in The Grange. These brothers were descended from the same family as Jane Seymour the third wife of King Henry VIII. In 1738 the well known Bath architect, John Wood lodged at The Grange. Across from The Grange is The Granchen, an 18th century coach house and stables which had belonged to The Grange. Beyond The Grange is the 16th century well constructed 'Dower House' set in beautiful gardens.

Church Farm, possibly the oldest house in the village, was formerly the Manor House remodelled in the 17th and 19th century.

Passing through the lych gate from the Church yard into Church Lane the old Vicarage can be seen on the right hand side. This was the residence of the Rev Henry Thomas Ellacombe, Vicar of Bitton from 1817 to 1850 and of his son Canon Henry Nicholson Ellacombe who was also Vicar of Bitton from 1850 to 1916, a total of 99 years between them. The house was built in two parts in 1778 and 1823. The Vicarage gardens became most famous as being one of the finest gardens in England. Other notable buildings surrounding the Church are the Frere's Almshouses built in 1859; the old Village School and Parish Room built in 1830 and the cottage at number 6 Church Lane which is of tudor – gothic origins and dates back to 1834.

Bitton used to have two Methodist Churches for worship. The Wesleyan Chapel, built in 1834 is no longer in existance but was situated in the High Street where Marley Automotive Components is today and the other, The United Methodist Free Church, now Bitton Methodist Church in Mill Lane. This Church has been an active fellowship serving the community since it was built in 1859.

Throughout this century there has certainly been no shortage of local industry, farming and nurseries in Bitton. Listed below are just some of those well known companies, farmers and nurserymen who have traded and served in the community:

INDUSTRIES –	Bush and Wilton	Engineers/Iron Founders
	Torrance & Sons Ltd	Engineers
	Golden Valley Paper Mills Ltd	Paper Manufacturers
	West of England Ochre & Oxide Co Ltd	Colour Manufacturers
	Caisley & Son	Furniture Manufacturers
	J C Dovey & Co	Colour Manufacturers
	John Govan	Motor Engineers
	Eustace Anstey	Motor Engineers
	Gilbert Ollis	Corn Merchant
FARMERS –	W Davis	Field Grove
	J T Dare	Lower Cullyhall
	B Fair	Upper Cullyhall
	Miss A Evans	Boyd Farm
	A Hawkins	Church Farm
	L J Ogborne	Redfield Farm
	S Perrett	Meadow Farm
	F Sparrow	Rock House
	F E Bungay	Westover Farm
		Hill Farm
		Knights Folly
NURSERYMEN –	J W Brighton	
	H G Gallop	
	A Lockwood	
	Fonthill Nurseries and Scotts Ltd	

Over the years the closures of both the Golden Valley Paper Mills and Torrances' affected employment both in the village and throughout the locality generally. It is pleasing, however to see, particularly over recent years that these premises have been re-occupied with new industries. Marley Automotive Components, previously British

Moulded Fibre, now occupy the former Golden Valley Paper Mills and Edward Brothers Environmental Services Ltd and Confidential Destruction Co (Bristol) Ltd have taken over the former Torrance Engineering premises. The well known Bush and Wilton Engineering Company is still well in evidence and has served the area outstandingly for over 200 years at their premises in Golden Valley Lane.

The various shops in the village have always served a very useful purpose, not only supplying the every day needs of the inhabitants, but also acting as a meeting place for the exchange of any local news. All those who have worked in the community have served the village well over the years, each with their own personality. It is always difficult to name individuals because all have played an important role but no doubt many will remember particularly, Doctor Thomas Aubrey of Westover House, who practised in the area from 1905 to 1945. Outside the gates of Westover House can be seen a stone plaque set in the wall by his patients and friends to commemorate his memory. 'Aubrey Meads' in the village was also named after him. 'Edwin Short Close' was named after Edwin (known as Harry) Short an active villager employed at Torrance & Son for over 40 years. Harry was also a member of the Church choir for many years and a keen cricketer until 1973. Mr Charles King-Smith who owned the Golden Valley Paper Mills was another well respected person in Bitton. He gave the village it's first street lighting and refuse collection. He also had little brick workshops built for some tenants who were cobblers or leather workers who previously worked in their kitchens, housing which was formerly the old pin factory.

Other notable features in the village are the village school, named 'The Meadows', The Recreation Club, and last but not least Bitton Railway Station now the Avon Valley Railway. More details of these will be given with the appropriate photograph.

'Time for a chat' on the corner of Kings Square, Bitton in 1908. At the top of the Square is located Hunters Hall built in 1833.
Photograph from M J Tozer Collection.

A summer scene on the same corner today. The shrubs and trees are well in evidence and the cottages, though hidden and modernised are still there.

The high Street pictured in 1908. Here we see the hub of the village with people doing their shopping. The pony and trap was a more quiet means of transport in those days.
Photograph from the M J Tozer Collection.

Bitton High Street today. Quite a busy street with plenty of traffic passing through between Bristol and Bath. The population of Bitton today is 1,800.

Another view of the High Street, going out of Bitton towards Bath, in the 1920's. On the left is the village store and the 'Kings Arms' which was owned by Bristol United Beers. Amongst the vehicles parked on the road is one of Stanley Ford's vans who was the Butcher from Oldland and further along the road is a motor bike and sidecar, a form of transport used regularly well into the 1950's.
Photograph from the M J Tozer Collection.

Today the Post Office is well in evidence on the left and the 'Kings Arms' licenced premises is replaced by the 'Spar Shop'.

154 – 162 High Street pictured on the left of the photograph is a two storey terrace built in 1767. They were used as a poor house for the village and later as a Pin Factory. The two smaller cottages to the left were once the village constable's house and lock up or 'jail house'. Parked outside the former Pin Factory is a well used form of transport of that time circa 1920 – the pony and trap. Possibly a local trader delivering his goods.
M J Tozer collection.

Today's photograph of the same buildings with Charles Stephens of Church Lane.

St Mary's Church – The Parish Church of Bitton pictured in 1908. A splendid building with a fine 14th century tower which forms a local landmark visible across the nearby Avon meadows.
M J Tozer Collection.

A view of the Church today in 1993. St Mary's is situated in a quiet corner away from the ever busy main road. The lane leading to the Church and the surrounding historic buildings is certainly a 'pathway into History'.

The former Wesleyan Methodist Chapel, built in 1834, situated in the High Street. Photographed in the 1930's, it closed as a Place of Worship and was later demolished in the middle of the century.
M J Tozer Collection.

The only reminder of where the old Weslyan Chapel stood is the stone indicating it's name and when it was built. The area is now used by Marley Automotive Components.

The White Hart Public House in the High Street. A Georges House photographed in 1955.
Photograph courtesy of Ken Thomas of Courages Ltd.

The Pub as it is today. Jenny Powell, the Landlady is pictured with her dog 'Ginny' at the entrance to The White Hart which also has a restaurant and family garden.

The former 'Rising Sun' Public House in Bath Road photographed in 1955, the year of its closure. It was owned by Bath Brewery Ltd until 1923 when it was then taken over by Georges of Bristol. Well known Landlords in the Pub during the 1920/40's was the Bristow family and in the 1940/50's was the Pearce family.
Photograph courtesy of Ken Thomas of Courage Ltd.

A modernised private residence has taken the place of the former 'Rising Sun'.

Pupils outside the 'new' Bitton Council School in Bath Road pictured in 1910 a year after the school was built.
M J Tozer Collection

Pupils of Class 6, Years 5/6, Miss Guwy's class, in the same position today. Now renamed 'The Meadows' the school has 175 pupils on the register and the Headmaster is Mr Warr.

Bitton Railway Station in 1908. The train pulling into the station has come from Oldland Common and is going towards Bath. For those keen train enthusiasts it is the 890 Class 2–4–0 No 89.
M J Tozer Collection.

Avon Valley Railway – Bitton Station today. Pictured on the platform in the fore ground is a young railway enthusiast, Craig Scott.
Photograph by the author.

Bitton Paper Mills

Golden Valley Paper Mills – 1910. The Paper Mill was the centre of industry for many years during this century in Bitton. It employed many people from within and around the area. Here we can also see the Mill pond which was surrounded by the River Boyd and the Mill on two sides and the Withy bed, rushes and hedge on the others. At times swans could be seen nesting safely out in the bulrushes along with the moor hens.
Photograph supplied by Roy Stone of Cadbury Heath

Today this building is used for an active industry owned by Marley Automotive Components. Sadly the pond has disappeared along with the swans and moor hens.
Photograph by the author.

Captain Ronald King-Smith, Director of the Golden Valley Paper Mills showing Her Majesty Queen Mary around the 'Top Saw' department when Her Royal Highness visited the factory in the 1940's.
Photographs supplied by Mildred Tarrant of Oldland Common.

Mildred Tarrant (Nee Pullin) pictured with H.R.H. Queen Mary and Captain Ronald King-Smith in the 'Top Saw' department.

Some of the women workers of The Golden Valley Paper Mill photographed in the early 1930's.
Photograph supplied by Ernest Phelps of Oldland Common.

Extract from 'More Memories of the Paper Mill' by Edna Nelmes ". . . we have just walked through the heat and noise of the drier and seen that wispy mixture become paper in large rolls about 6ft. wide and 18ins. in diameter and now we walk down a slope into the bottom-saw. Here there were cutting machines which were adjusted to the size required, and lovely quality paper flowed down to collect in neat piles, later to be stacked on wooden platforms and then up in the lift to the top-saw. Here the office took samples for quality control and girls sorted the paper. They wore a rubber hood on the middle finger of their right hand and, working in facing pairs and surprisingly swiftly, flipped sheets off the pile. The perfect paper jiggled against bricks covered with paper – the sheets marked in any way were tweaked out proud, then at intervals, jerked right out and thrown on the pile at the side to be thrown in the bins for re-cycling. . ."

Villagers of Bitton join in the celebrations on VE Day in 1945. This photograph taken in Cherry Gardens, shows many who are either still resident or live around the surrounding area of the village today.
Photograph supplied by Gordon Neal formerly of Bitton and now of High Street, Oldland Common.

111

The Frere's Almshouses in Church Lane. These houses are situated in a most interesting and historical area of Bitton. They were built in 1859 with the motto 'Frere Ayme Frere' ('Brother Loves Brother') inscribed over the first floor window head. A 1993 photograph shows the author talking to Mrs Joyce Gerrish, one of the occupants, who has lived in the area all her life and who served on the Parish Council for over 25 years.

Aubrey Meads, off Golden Valley Lane in Bitton, as it is today. It was named after Doctor Thomas Aubrey who practised and served in the community for 40 years.

BITTON AND IT'S COMMUNITY

Bitton Recreation Club in Bath Road – 1950. The Club, situated on the Recreation Field was given to the village of Bitton in 1918 by Mr Charles King-Smith, a Director of The Golden Valley Paper Mills. The building was formerly an ex-army Nissan Hut which was purchased from Salisbury Plain directly after the first World War. Many organised activities were held in the Club including concerts, and directly before and after the 2nd World War the premises were used as the local library. The YMCA or Red Triangle Club was first involved in the Club in 1945 and remained there for several years.
M J Tozer Collection

Outside the Bitton Club on a warm summer's day in June of this year, 1993. David Venables, the Club Steward was busy working inside the building but was persuaded to be in our photgraph on virtually the same spot as the Steward or member (name not known) had stood in the previous photograph taken some 43 years earlier.

Senior Class of Bitton Council School in 1945 photographed with the popular Headmaster, Mr Percy Townend who served the School for well over 20 years. He also served faithfully on the Warmley Rural District Council for many years.
Photograph supplied by Gordon Neal of High Street, Oldland Common, pictured 5th from the right on the middle row.

'The Meadows' School, formerly Bitton Council School, Under 12s Rugby Football Team 1993. Runners up in the Kingswood Festival.
Photograph courtesy of John Channing, Pickwick Portraits of Keynsham.

Bitton Cricket Club photographed in 1950. Back row; Mr Melhuish, Keith Short, Dave Duckett, Chris Marsh, Charlie Hurst, Jack Bracey, Steve Townend and George Hurst.
Front row; Ken Bisp, Peter Hurst, John West, Gordon Neal and Jack Hunt.
Photograph supplied by Charlie Hurst of Aubrey Meads, Bitton and the following information kindly supplied by Gordon Neal, Chairman of Bitton Recreation and Cricket Club.

Bitton Cricket Club was established in 1851. The first 'recorded' game was against Corsham on the 14th September 1855. The first 'home' games were played on 'the Meadows' behind the Church. Canon Ellacombe became the first President of the club in 1897 and since that time there have only been 5 other people who have served in that capacity. From 1898 to 1918 the teams played in a field by the 'Rising Sun' Public House and from 1920 both the Cricket Club and Bitton Tennis Club began playing on the recreation field commonly known as 'The Rec'. In 1923 Bitton Football Club also commenced playing their matches there.

The combined Football Teams and officials of Bitton and Cadbury Heath photographed in 1949/50 on the steps outside the Bitton Recreation Club before the start of one of the many 'local derby' games played over the years between the two teams.
Photograph supplied by Gordon Neal of High Street, Oldland Common.

Bitton Football Club – Players, officials and mascots photographed before the start of a match in 1954.
Photograph supplied by Gordon Neal of High Street, Oldland Common.

Players, officials and guests photographed at the Presentation Dinner of Bitton Football Club, Bristol and District Division 3, 1955/56 season.
Photograph supplied by Gordon Neal of High Street, Oldland Common.

BITTON AND THE GREAT FLOOD OF 1968

The night Bitton and the West was turned upside down
Wednesday July 10th 1968 – 25 years ago

Many Bitton villagers will no doubt remember the Great Flood of 1968 which brought devastation on a scale unparalleled in the South West.

It started to rain on the evening of Wednesday July 10th accompanied by heavy thunder and lightning. The rain continued to fall with incessant fury for a day and a night without pause. It was a night when the elements turned against local villagers leaving them weary, depressed and despairing. At daybreak on Thursday, July 11th, the full extent of the floods was seen. Many surrounding villages were also badly effected. The following photographs show just how the village of Bitton and its residents were shattered by this horrific experience on that Wednesday night 25 years ago.

'Bitton in the Floods of 1968.' This car finds it hard going in the flooded High Street of Bitton in July 1968. The White Hart Public House is in the background.
Photograph courtesy of Bristol Observer.

117

Heather Linton of 5 Mill Rank, throws out a bowl of water as she mops up after the floods. Surrounding her is the furniture from her devastated home.
Photograph courtesy of Bristol Observer.

Paddling day for the youngsters after the heavy rains in 1968.
Photograph courtesy of Bristol Observer.

'A BITTON BOY LOOKS BACK'
by
Terry Jefferies
of
Bath Road, Bitton

Terry and Shirley Jefferies

I was born in 1936, one of the seven children of James and Mabel Jefferies. We were brought up in Mill House, Bitton, which was owned by the Golden Valley Paper Mills. The Directors of the Mills were the King-Smith family and they were responsible for one of the main industries of the village having been in business from 1903 to around the middle of the century.

At the age of five I attended Bitton Council School, now named The Meadows, in Bath Road. These were the days of the second World War when life was very different from today. Food was rationed and for some families it was quite often a struggle to make ends meet. The village, however, had a strong community spirit and neighbours and friends were always on hand to help each other out in times of need.

As children we used to enjoy ourselves making our own fun and games in the streets and on the various farmers fields surrounding the village. My father, James, was employed as a Blacksmith in the Paper Mills for over 30 years and with mum lived the latter end of their lives in the Alms Houses in Church Lane.

I remained at Bitton Council School until I was 14 years old and then went on to the Seniors at Oldland Secondary Modern School for 1 year before leaving to take up a five year apprenticeship with Torrance Engineering Company. I was with this Company until 1959 when I then joined J S Fry & Sons, now Cadbury Ltd. as a Maintenance Fitter.

Bitton in the early to mid century was a close knit community and looking back as a boy and then in the succeeding years, many of the old family names come to mind – ALWAY, AUBREY, BRACEY, BREWER, BRISTOW, BUSH, CARY, CAVILL, CLARK, COLES, COUNSELL, DUCKETT, FISHER, FORD, GAY, GALLOP, GERRISH, GREADY, HOBBS, HOOPER, HUNT, HURST, ISAACS, JEFFERIES, JONES, KING, MOON, MULLINS, NEAL, PEARCE, PERRETT, PULLIN, ROBBINS, SELMAN, SHORT, STEADMAN, TARRANT, TOWNEND, WATTS, WILLIS, WILTON and WOOD. Each made their own impression and contribution to our village life. Apologies for any names omitted!

During my lifetime in Bitton it has always been a very 'sporting' village. The Recreation field in Bath Road has been a centre of activity particularly for the Football and Cricket Teams which have played at a high standard and been a main attraction. I remember playing football for the 1st Bitton Boys Team at the age of 15. Bitton Recreation Social Club has served the community well over many years with a variety of entertainment. The building was previously a Nissan Hut brought from Salisbury Plain in Wiltshire. The present chairman of the Bitton Recreation and Cricket Club is Gordon Neal and the Chairman of Bitton Club and Ground Association is Jack Gready. Having lived in the village for many years, both as a youngster growing up and after my marriage to Shirley and having our own three children, it is inevitable that one would see many changes in the life of the village. Looking back over the years perhaps one of the biggest changes I have seen concerns the employment of the residents of the village. During the 1940's to 60's about 90% of the people in Bitton would have found employment within the village itself whereas now most of the residents are employed in Companies outside of the village. On the whole the changes made in the village have been necessary for progress and it is pleasing to say that it has still maintained it's friendly atmosphere. However, gone are the days when the door was left on 'the latch' with neighbours just walking in and horse drawn carts delivering milk cannot be seen along the Bath Road today!

As a 'Bitton Boy' I have many happy memories and I trust that by sharing these and looking back it will bring as much nostalgia to others, present and former residents of Bitton as it has for me.

LISTED BUILDINGS IN THE LOCALITY

During my research for material around the various villages featured in this publication many people have asked me if I had any information about the listed buildings of the area. 'Listed buildings' are buildings of special architectural or historic interest given protection, not afforded to other buildings, under the Town and County Planning Act. They are graded as follows:

GRADE I – Buildings of exceptional interest – less than 5% of the National total of listed buildings are in this category.

GRADE II* – Particularly outstanding Grade II buildings.

GRADE II – Buildings of special interest which warrant every effort being made to preserve them.

LOCAL LIST – Normally prepared by the Borough or District Council.
Although it does not give buildings the legal protection provided by the main list, it identifies other distinctive old buildings worthy of special attention.

Indicated below is a breakdown of the number of buildings throughout the area and categorised accordingly.

	GRADE I	GRADE II*	GRADE II	LOCALLY LISTED
OLDLAND COMMON	NIL	NIL	15	48
NORTH COMMON	NIL	NIL	NIL	7
BRIDGEYATE	NIL	NIL	12	3
BITTON	1 (St Mary's Church)	4	52	26

POSTSCRIPT

I trust that these reminiscings and the information given in this book have been of interest to all readers. Hopefully it is the first in a series of publications about the local area, so I would be very pleased to receive any comments or to hear from readers who may have any material, photographs or information, particularly on local dates for the 'through the decades', for future publications.

There is possibly some information which readers may have thought should have been included in this first edition, if so perhaps you would either like to write down your thoughts or reminiscings about your area or let me come and chat with you about them. I would be only too pleased to hear from you.

Siston, Webbs Heath, Swineford, Willsbridge, Upton Cheyney, Beach and North Stoke are possible villages to be covered in future publications plus any additional material on Oldland Common, North Common, Bridgeyate and Bitton. There must be many photographs about these areas tucked away somewhere and many memories just waiting to be written down. Please contact me if you can help in any way.

BIBLIOGRAPHY

County History 1779 – Samuel Rudder.

Kelly's Directory of Gloucestershire 1906.

A Brief History of Oldland, compiled in the mid 1950's by Miss G E Burns – a former Postmistress of Oldland.

John Wesley's Journal – 1761.

Hold the Front Page by James Belsey, Bristol United Press Ltd, (Redcliffe Press) 1992.

Chronicle Communications Ltd.

Ordnance Survey.

Readers Digest.

Kingswood Heritage Trail – Kingswood Borough Council Planning Dept.

Bridgeyate Church 175th Anniversary – I H Dearnley 1985.

History of the Parish of Bitton – Reverend Henry Thomas Ellacombe 1881.

Memories of the 'Golden Valley Paper Mill' – Edna Nelmes.